I0775204

MAGIC SOUP, TYPING MONKEYS, AND HORNY ALIENS FROM OUTER SPACE:

The Patently Absurd
Wholly Unsubstantiated
and
Extravagantly Failed

Atheist Origin Myth

by

EVAN SAYET

Copyright © 2023, Evan Sayet
All Rights Reserved

To my parents Lucille and Gene Sayet with gratitude for the past; my children with love in the present, and my grandson with every hope for the future.

TABLE OF CONTENTS

PREFACE

Although I wouldn't come to realize it for many years, my journey from New York City-born, non-believing Jew, in the entertainment industry in Hollywood, California to New York City-born, believing Jew, writing this book in Dallas, Texas, began with an appearance by the famed "evolutionary biologist," Richard Dawkins, on a television show, *Politically Incorrect with Bill Maher*, that I had been writing for many years.

Dawkins is an avid and outspoken atheist and, while at the time I agreed with his conclusion, there was something about his performance that night that I'd found rather disturbing. In retrospect, it wasn't just that night, either. It was whenever he, or any of the other aggressively atheistic guests, appeared on the show.

Whether it was those who held scientific credentials like Dawkins, those who fancied themselves "intellectuals" like Christopher Hitchens, or a comedian like Maher who was assaulting what other people believe about God's existence, there was a certain smugness – often a smarminess, really – that I found rather unbecoming of those claiming the mantle of moral, intellectual, and scientific superiority.

What I kept noticing was that, for all of their scientific credentials, intellectual bona fides and comedic chops, there was surprisingly little science, intellect, or wit to their efforts. On that night, for example, rather than the disciplined precision one expects of a scientific argument, Dawkins was hyperbolic and emotional and, as I would more and more come to learn, both light on and loose with the facts.

For his part, Hitchens was typically rambling and over-the-top and, as it turns out, often intoxicated. As for Maher, rather than the clever turn-of-a-phrase or ironic twist that defines a joke, Maher's attacks on that night and others were never anything more than verbal cruelties masquerading as humor, and always devoid of any actual substance. At some point it became undeniable to me that that, for some reason, we atheists could ridicule, but we could never actually refute.

At the same time that I was noticing the dearth of seriousness in the atheists' assaults on the beliefs of others,

I began to recognize the absence of any scientific argument on behalf of any alternative. We atheists could tell you what it is that we *didn't* believe about the origin of the universe and the design found everywhere within it; but we would never even try to tell you what it is that we *do* believe in God's stead.

As it turns out, there's good reason that atheists don't ever attempt to argue on behalf of their scientific beliefs. It's because atheism is not a scientific belief. In fact, atheism is neither scientific; nor is it a belief.

Simply disbelieving one thing does not in any way suggest a belief in anything else. Atheists don't believe in God, but neither do they believe in any of the alternatives. The atheists simply ignore the questions of origin and design as if they don't exist.

The atheists, of course, will insist that they believe in "science;" but all they mean by that, is that they don't believe in God. In fact, when offered the opportunity to share the science that they say that they believe in, even Dawkins will, at best, hem and hew for maybe a second or two, before instantly returning to attacking the beliefs of others.

Meanwhile, failing to rise to the level of a belief, atheism thus fails to rise to the level of science. Science – real science – requires more than the mere out-of-hand dismissal of a theory one doesn't personally like. Science – real science – requires that an alternative theory be proposed that better answers the various questions presented by the realities of our physical existence.

As it turns out, not only do the atheists' theories about the various Big Questions fail to provide better answers than does the God hypothesis; the atheists are yet to have even offered a single legitimate theory regarding any of the Big Questions. Not one. Not even about just one small part. The atheist disbelieves in God, but can offer no science either to refute the God hypothesis or to support any alternative. That is not science.

The problem for the atheists is not that they haven't *yet* come up with a theory; it's that there is and cannot be any alternative to the God hypothesis that fits the limited definition of "science" that the atheists have imposed in order to disqualify God as an acceptable belief.

If theories about an intelligent creator cannot be considered acceptable because God is outside of the materials, forces, and physical laws of our universe and/or beyond the four dimensions of height, width, depth, and time in which we humans can perceive, then no theory can be considered acceptable because it is simply a fact that the universe came from beyond the materials, forces, and physical laws of our world and/or beyond our four dimensions.

It's really quite simple. Given that the universe is here; there are only two possibilities. Either it was always here or it wasn't always here. Period. That's it. The problem for the atheists is that, if it's the former, then it is unacceptable because it is outside of the dimension of time. If it's the latter, it's unacceptable because the universe would have had to have come from materials, forces, and laws emanating from outside of our own. There are only two possibilities and both of them are "antiscientific" according to the limited definition of "science" the atheists use to disqualify the God hypothesis.

Further, since "it was just somehow always here" is not even a theory about the origin and design of the universe – and, oh, yeah, Einstein disproved it over a hundred years ago, anyway – there is only one scientific possibility left: the universe came from outside of the materials, laws, and forces found in our world.

The only question left, then, is: was our universe intentionally designed and created or was its creation a matter of luck and its design the result of happenstance?

Since the answer is, by definition, beyond our science and abilities to perceive, we will likely never know the answer with certitude. Fortunately, science – real science – doesn't tend to deal in certitudes. Science – real science – demands only that the theory that better answers the various questions that physical reality poses be embraced.

This book looks at the two and only two possible answers – both of them "extra-scientific" – and weighs what science knows (and doesn't know) about the origin of the universe and the design of the things that are in it. It focuses on both the "science" of atheism, as well as the politics of the Militant Atheist movement, that has turned atheism from a personal belief into an ideological movement. By the end, I think it will be rather clear why it is that the atheists ridicule but don't refute; and why it is that after ten thousand years they have failed to even conjure a theory about even just one small part of even just one of the Big Questions.

INTRODUCTION

We take the side of science in spite of the patent absurdity of some of its constructs, in spite of its failure to fulfill many of its extravagant promises...and in spite of the tolerance of the scientific community for unsubstantiated just-so stories because we have a prior commitment, a commitment to materialism

– Harvard "evolutionary biologist" and famed Militant Atheist, Richard Lewontin writing in the
New York Review of Books

"Militant Atheist" is not a term I just coined for the occasion. It is, in fact, what the *Wall Street Journal* has dubbed a new breed of professional Atheists – people like Richard Dawkins, Sam Harris, Steven Pinker, Daniel Dennett, and Richard Lewontin – who call themselves "scientists" but who, in reality, have made a career out of nothing more than using the color of their titles and the cachet and power of their positions to aggressively evangelize, sermonize, and proselytize in an effort to expunge God from society.

I hate to break it to Dr. Lewontin and the others, but when someone embraces and promotes constructs that they know to be patently absurd, makes promises that, time and again, have proved to have been extravagant in both their telling and in their failures, and "tolerates" stories that are "just-so" in their narrative and unsubstantiated in their evidence, one is not taking the side of science. One is, in fact, betraying it.

Scientists – real scientists – have no prior commitments to anything other than to the truth. Scientists – real scientists – go wherever it is that the facts lead, even if it is in utter opposition to their most deeply cherished personal, religious, financial, and/or political obligations.

When one's commitment is to anything other than to the truth, one is not a scientist; one is, in fact, a propagandist. Throughout history, whenever the claims of the propagandists have become the "official science" – no matter how noble the cause may or may not have seemed at the time – it has never turned out well for humanity. Never. As we shall see, it doesn't this time, either.

What's most disturbing about Dr. Lewontin's confession is that it wasn't whispered conspiratorially in some backroom, nor was it offered with even the slightest hint of contrition. Quite to the contrary; it was stated as a simple matter of course in the highly prestigious, and sometimes even read, *New York Review of Books*.

Lewontin called the cause for which he so nonchalantly admits to betraying not merely his own profession but also all of the people who then count on the word of these "scientists" to make the most profound decisions in their own lives "materialism," but in reality "materialism" is nothing other than the "unofficial official" euphemism that professional Atheists use to make their ideological agenda appear less obvious. "Materialism" is simply the word that the Militants use when they mean to say "atheism."

Had Lewontin been more fully honest in his confession, then it would have read something more like:

> *We Militant Atheists who call ourselves "scientists" take the side of atheism despite its patent absurdities, extravagantly failed promises, and wholly unsubstantiated just-so stories, because our loyalty to the truth is trumped by a commitment to our political cause.*

"Materialism" is defined as the belief (or the stated belief) that "nothing exists except matter" and clearly the fact that this matter even matters proves that there's more to the universe than just physical matter. The fact that we're thinking about it and that our thoughts, then, lead to actions and that those actions, then, have real-world consequences makes undeniable that more than just mere matter matters.

This matter matters quite a lot to the Militants. It matters so much to them, in fact, that they're willing to betray their profession and lie to those who trust them the most in order to promote what is, in fact, not a scientific belief, but an ideological crusade.

Just what it is that these Militants seek to achieve through their efforts is the subject of my previous works, *The KinderGarden of Eden* and *The Woke Supremacy* (and will be revisited in the final chapters here) but for now it is far less important to agree on the purpose of their lies, than it is to acknowledge – just as Lewontin has acknowledged – that they do, in fact, lie and that the reason that they lie is the very same reason that anyone else does: the truth simply does not comport to what it is they want others to believe.

Obviously, the bigger the lies and the more often they're told, the further from the truth are the individual's claims. One would be hard-pressed, then, to even imagine bigger lies more often told than constructs that are known to be patently absurd, promises that are understood to be extravagant both in their making and then in their failures, and "just-so" stories conjured wholly without substantiation, all then repeated as simply so much a matter of course that one need not fear even the slightest professional repercussions for admitting to them in even the most public and widely distributed of forums.

That these lies are then sold to a trusting public as "settled science," with their mere questioning instantly rendering one a "religious zealot" to be rejected out of hand, feared and righteously silenced, makes these lies only that much more egregious – and dangerous – still.

If you are of the belief that science has answered all of the Big Questions of creation and design and, in having done so, has left the God of the Bible in the pile of discarded superstitions, folklore, legends, and myths of the past, you could not possibly be more mistaken. That's understandable, though; you've been lied to. With big lies. Oft told. As simply a matter of course. The professional Atheists nothing less than admit to doing just that, and they do so in even the most public of settings.

What you will find in these coming pages is what I have found: far from the Atheists having answered all of the Big Questions about creation and design, they haven't even the very first clue as to even a single part of even just one of them.

The problem isn't that the professional Atheists don't know the science – they know it extremely well. The problem is that all known science, across every known field of science, as well as literally every observation, discovery, and experiment – you know, what real scientists call "data" – going all the way back to the very first day of the world's very first caveman, at once so fully supports the theory of Intelligent Design in general and the existence of the God of the Bible in particular, and, at the same time, so totally debunks its any and every possible materialistic alternative, that even the Atheists themselves are forced to admit that they cannot even conjure a theory about even just any one small part of even just one of the Big Questions about creation and design, that isn't known to them to be patently absurd, wholly unsubstantiated, and extravagantly failed in its every promise.

CHAPTER ONE

THE ORIGIN OF THE UNIVERSE

To give you an idea of just how little scientific evidence there is that supports the Atheist hypothesis of a Godless origin to the universe, simply consider a conversation I had with my friend Edward Tryon, the Hunter College physics professor considered by many to have been the intellectual heir to Albert Einstein.

Tryon had just been asked to write an article for the then, still relevant, *Time* magazine as it celebrated Einstein as its "Person of the Century," explaining in laymen's terms the best theory today's Materialists have for how the universe might have first come into existence.

Tryon's paper was an absolutely brilliantly written, several page long treatise, that concluded with the following words:

I humbly propose to you that the universe is simply one of those things that just happens from time to time.

The next time I saw Ed, I said to him, "You do realize that your conclusion is simply a more polite way of saying 'shit happens!', don't you?" Ed slumped his shoulders, dropped his head, and said with chagrin, "Yeah."

"Shit happens!" is not a scientific hypothesis; it's what a clueless stoner says when he spills his energy drink on your vinyl collection. In fact, not only is "shit happens!" not a scientific hypothesis, it is the very opposite of one. It's an admission that, when it comes to the question at hand, there is simply no reasonable scientific explanation in the offing.

Yet one more of the world's leading scientists – an heir to Einstein no less – joins with Lewontin and the others Lewontin refers to in his article as "we," in acknowledging that today's Materialists are no closer to a good explanation for the existence of the universe than were the pre-Enlightenment Greeks and Romans with their own unsubstantiated myths and patently absurd origin stories or, for that matter, the world's very first caveman to have peered off into the night sky, pointed in dumb wonder, and grunted "Ugg!"

This is because, in the words of the famed historian, Paul Johnson: "The modern world began on May 29th, 1919, when photographs of a solar eclipse confirmed the truth of a new theory of the universe."

It was on that day, over a hundred years ago, that Einstein's theory of General Relativity went from brilliant conjecture into accepted science. It remains, more than a century later, the "standard model" across every relevant scientific field and the very thing that first helped to usher in the scientific and technological boom that continues to this day.

One of the things that was proved on that day is that the universe and everything in it – matter, energy, space, and time – had a beginning. This fact was utterly devastating to the Atheists for it, at once, proved the most essential element behind the theory of Intelligent Design to be true and, at the same time, it rendered any materialistic alternative – the only possible alternatives – not merely wrong but impossible.

If, as Einstein had proved, matter and energy didn't exist before the "Big Bang" that began the universe, then obviously these things cannot be the explanation for how they first came into being. As Stephen Meyer, author of *The Return of the God Hypothesis* notes:

> *Clearly matter and energy could not have caused themselves to come into existence before they existed.*

Scientists use an ancient word with a Latin root to explain the logic behind this conclusion: they say, "duh." It is simply self-evident that that which did not yet exist could not have been the cause of its own existence. Duh.

This obvious and undeniable fact has left the Atheists wholly incapable of offering even a theory which would then fall within the Materialists' own definition of "science" and, to this day, save for a now-mumbled "Shit happens" – and on some Boston area campuses a grunted "Ugg" – they still haven't.

All these years later, the Atheists still have no better theory to explain the origin of the universe without God than the fact that "shit happens;" something that, no doubt, even the world's very first caveman was equally well-aware of. In fact, several recent linguistic studies suggest that, when translated into English, "Ugg" actually means "shit happens."

Making matters even worse for the Atheists is that not only did Einstein's theory prove the most essential element behind the theory of Intelligent Design to be true, but it also made a second essential element of that theory the only reasonable conclusion.

As legendary astrophysicist Robert Jastrow, nothing less than the founding director of NASA's Goddard Institute for Space Studies put it, if the universe was created, "then there simply has to have been a creator." Duh. (Duh is conjugated in its original Latin as duhus, duhex, duhem.)

There is simply no known law or laws of physics – or any of the other known sciences for that matter – that allows for creation without a creator. Even if someday scientists were somehow able to conjure some or another theory that allowed for something to come from nothing, it still wouldn't save the Materialists. If one's entire theory is based on the doctrine that only matter matters, then just how the immaterial created the material is wholly immaterial. Duh, yet again!

Here's where it starts to get really interesting, though. As if things could possibly get any worse for the Atheists, it turns out that Einstein wasn't the only one to have been proved right on that day. Some three thousand years before science first began to embrace the concepts in Einstein's theory, the Hebrew Bible started with the astonishing declaration that time had had a beginning and, just as impressively, that, just as Einstein had rightly theorized, it was almost immediately followed by a big explosion of light.

These now accepted scientific facts didn't appear in some footnote or codicil in the Bible, nor are they open to any other possible interpretations. They are, in fact, the very first words in that ancient text – "In the beginning" and

"Let there be light" – stated unambiguously and sworn to by millions of Christians and Jews for thousands of years before scientists finally began to swear to them as well.

Even the one thing that the Atheists used and continue to use most in their efforts to try and disparage those who believe in a literal interpretation of the Bible – those the professional Atheists derisively call the "Young Earthers" (of which I am not one) – was given a degree of plausibility by Einstein's having proved that time is relative.

If time is relative, then the "days" and "years" referred to in the Bible are merely units of time and, when taken as such, they once again prove those first Hebrews to have been stunningly accurate, this time with regard to both the order and the duration of creation.

In fact, in the book *The Genesis Enigma: Why the First Book of the Bible is Scientifically Accurate,* Cambridge University-educated biologist Andrew Parker walks us through each of the "days" of creation and the order that scientists now know the advent of the universe, the finetuning of the cosmos, and the progression of life on earth to have occurred and they are, in fact, just as the Bible states at every turn and in every way.

Perhaps the poetic imagery, metaphor and allegory of some of the Bible's later stories is not to your personal liking, but there is simply no denying that what science now knows about the origin of the universe and all of the things in it, comports to perfection and in every way to those very first few pages of that ancient Hebrew text.

The Bible didn't just get the science right, though. There can be no such thing as science without a God just like the one in the Bible. This is because a monotheistic God is the first – and only – requirement for the existence of science itself.

This doesn't mean that previous cultures (or those with either no god or many gods today) couldn't accomplish scientific tasks. They could and they did. What it means is that the methodical study of science – the Scientific Method – would be an impossibility without a singular God just like the one the Jews first introduced to the world.

With no God, there could be no laws of science because there would have been no one and nothing to have created them. The laws of our science couldn't have been created by the laws of our science for the simple reason that that which did not yet exist could not have been the cause of its own existence. Duh.

At the same time, while multiple Gods might have been able to have created laws, those laws wouldn't have been consistent. The *constants* upon which the Scientific Method relies would be an impossibility with multiple, capricious, and competing gods for the simple reason that those laws would have then been multiple, capricious, and competing. Double Duh.

"Duh," it should be noted, is the very opposite of a patent absurdity. This is what scientists call a "*double*-duh!" The Latin word for patent absurdities is "huh?" (Conjugated in its original Latin as huhus, huhex, huhem.)

That the laws of our sciences are in fact constant – and constant throughout the entirety of the universe and across the whole of time – is yet one more essential scientific truth first revealed in the Bible's earliest pages in utter opposition to all previously held beliefs, both scientific and religious. It, too, is something that science would then take millennia to only, then, first confirm for itself.

The laws and constants of science, the standard model of the universe, the structuring of the cosmos and the correct order of how life progressed on earth; that's not a bad start. And we're still only on the very first few pages of the very first book of monotheism's very first text. Meanwhile, three thousand years later, the Atheists are still stuck on "Ugg!"

For the Atheists, Einstein's having confirmed the science of the Bible was utterly shattering. In fact, Jastrow described the feeling amongst them at the time as being nothing less than like a nightmare:

> *For the scientist who has lived by his faith in reason, the story ends like a bad dream. He has scaled the mountains of ignorance; he is about to conquer the highest peak; as he pulls himself over the final rock, he is greeted by a band of theologians who have been sitting there for centuries.*

Actually, though, it wasn't just centuries; it was millennia. And it wasn't just clever "theologians" deeply pondering and bandying about multiple and competing theories as they sipped brandy in their churches and universities. It was Western Civilization's very first theologians – a band of likely illiterate slaves escaping their tormentors as they struggled for survival in the unforgiving desert. *These* are the folks, folks, whose scientific theories Einstein and others would later fully confirm, even as the Atheists continue to just point and grunt in desperation.

With these basic and essential scientific truths still the very basis of science itself, far from the Judeo-Christian God being merely a "god of the gaps" whose majesty shrinks with each new scientific find, it is actually Atheistic "science" that has grown ever more implausible – patently absurd, really, as Lewontin admits – at its each and every turn.

As each and every new scientific discovery has revealed only an ever-greater complexity and an ever more stunning precision to the workings of the universe and each and all of the things in it, the odds that it all "somehow" "just happened" to have "somehow" "just happened" by luck and for no reason grows ever more unlikely.

At the same time, every new Atheistic theory that even attempts to explain the phenomena by anything other than luck, only sees the Militants forced to move ever closer to the theory of Intelligent Design in general and the God of the Bible in particular.

Prominent amongst these latest Atheistic efforts are such things as the "multiverse" and "string theory." The former postulates that there are *universes* outside of our own where the laws of our sciences don't apply. The latter argues that there are *dimensions* beyond the mere four in which we humans can perceive.

The idea that there are universes with laws outside of our own and/or dimensions in which we humans can't perceive is exactly what the science of Intelligent Design and the Bible postulate, and the very thing that the Atheists use to disqualify the God hypothesis as "not scientific" in the first place.

Take a moment and let this sink in: the very thing that the Atheists use to disqualify the God hypothesis as "not scientific," is now the Atheist scientists' most widely embraced belief. In fact, since "shit happens" is not actually a theory, what the science of Intelligent Design and the Bible postulates is now the Atheists only remaining theory.

As it turns out, then, there is no difference – no difference whatsoever – between what the two sides accept to be the known facts, nor is there any difference between what it is that the known facts lead the two sides to believe.

Both the Materialists and those who embrace the science of Intelligent Design agree that all known science, across every known field of science, as well as literally every observation, discovery and experiment – you know, what real scientists call "data" – going all the way back to the very first day of the world's very first caveman, makes undeniable that the universe and everything in it could not have been created by the materials, laws, and forces in our perceivable universe.

The only difference between those who embrace the science of Intelligent Design and those who are peddling "strings" and "multiverses," is found in how they each got there. The scientists behind the theory of Intelligent Design make their case in the affirmative. That is, they use the known science to show how it leads to a universe and/or dimensions beyond our own. I call this the "What is" method.

The Atheists, on the other hand, use what I call the "What if?" method whereby, recognizing that all known science has rendered any materialistic theory in this universe simply impossible, they simply decreed that there just have to be others, where the politically acceptable materialistic answers have all been hiding from them for the past ten thousand years.

There is no actual evidence for or any reason to believe in these patently absurd "vibrating strings;" nor is there evidence or reason to believe in the "multiverse" model the Atheists now cling to despite its being extravagantly failed in its every test. The professional Atheists simply made these things up and peddle them because they are the least-worst remaining theories after all known science has debunked their every less absurd efforts.

Whereas both the science of Intelligent design and the revelations of the Bible, then, have provided us with the laws and constants of science and, in fact, the very concept of science itself, the Atheists have so fully exhausted their search for any possible materialistic alternative to the God hypothesis in this universe and in these dimensions, that they've been forced to simply concede to the believers the existence of others. Beyond that, the only thing the Atheists have to say is "Ugg!"

25

CHAPTER TWO

IGOR, IT'S ALIVE!

With the Atheist "scientists" no further along in their understanding of the origin of the universe than was the world's very first caveman; they are once again running neck-and-neck with the Neanderthals when it comes to the question of how life might have first come from the insentient.

In fact, in an article published in the highly respected *Scientific American*, John Horgan sums up the state of Atheistic theory in just the title alone:

> *Psst! Don't Tell the Creationists, but Scientists Don't Have a Clue About How Life Began!*

Not even a clue. That, as it turns out, is *exactly* the same number of clues that the world's very first caveman had. On his very first day.

Dennis Overbye, the famed science writer for the *New York Times* (I'll wait while my atheist friends finish genuflecting), marveled at the same reality:

> *Geologists, chemists, astronomers, and biologists are as stumped as ever by the riddle of life.*

"As stumped as ever." As in ever. As in way back in the Stone Age ever. It's one thing to not believe the Bible, but this was in the *New York Times*!

Overbye's article was damning; but it did, however, contain one glaring error. It's not "scientists" who don't have a clue – in fact, scientists have, literally, every clue in the world. What Overbye meant, was only that the *Atheists* are as stumped as ever as to how life could possibly have begun *without God*. People who embrace the science behind the God hypothesis and the revelations of the Bible, aren't stumped at all.

The Materialists' failure is certainly not for a lack of trying. Today alone, tens of thousands of the world's greatest minds work diligently, night and day, and for years on end, trying to animate the inanimate. Standing on the shoulders of the giants of yore, using the most advanced, sophisticated, and carefully calibrated array of equipment, the best and the brightest at universities, private corporations, and both government and non-government agencies, in nations all across the globe toil around the clock towards this one end and still, the Materialists remain as stumped as ever. As in ever. As in the very first day of man on earth ever. At 12:01 a.m.

Particularly humiliating about the Atheists failures is that it really shouldn't be all that hard. After all, if what the Atheists claim took place in the vast dark void of the universe just by luck was actually true, they'd then be starting their crusade with every conceivable advantage.

Whereas the universe would have had to have started from scratch, and then created through the random interactions of insentient materials, all of the elements and forces that the Atheists say, then, "somehow" "just happened" to have arisen from the dead like it was John Travolta after the movie *Pulp Fiction* or something, all the Atheists would have to do is simply start at the very end of the process and just reverse engineer life as we know it, with every material, force, and tool needed all easily and readily at hand.

Further, whereas the universe would have had to have created life in the uncontrolled and uncontrollable vast, dark, cold, and ever-changing void of space, the Atheists' experiments are highly controlled, conducted in the most well-regulated of confines, in state-of-the-art facilities where they employ many and massive computers that run through the possibilities at staggering rates of speed. In fact, thanks to online delivery, they no longer even need to stop for lunch.

Even so, the Atheists today are no closer to a materialistic explanation for the advent of life than if they hadn't even begun their now ten-thousand-year long slog to nowhere and had, instead, just gone to see the movie *The Rocky Horror Picture Show*. As we shall see, the Atheists' latest, best, and in fact only remaining theory about how life might have begun on earth without God bears a striking resemblance to that patently absurd – although equally substantiated – sci-fi sex romp, even if the Atheists' choice of dress might sometimes be different.

Meanwhile, those Atheists who stake their hopes on the promise that someday, after ten thousand years of trying, one of their experiments might finally pay off and in doing so perhaps first begin to undermine the science of Intelligent Design in general and the revelations of the Bible in particular, fail to see the irony of their efforts.

Even if someday scientists were finally able to animate the inanimate, all that they will have then succeeded in doing is to have yet again reconfirmed the essential elements of the theory of Intelligent Design and the revelations found in the Bible.

Whatever "life" scientists might someday yet perhaps first coax from the dead will have required exactly those very things that the science of Intelligent Design and the Bible postulate: preexisting life (that of the scientists), with the intelligence in this case to have designed the precision experiments, protocols, machinery, tools, computers, and other equipment that they've employed – including the Uber Eats app – in their now millennia-long, and thus-far entirely and in every conceivable way failed, political crusade.

CHAPTER THREE

HORNY ALIENS FROM OUTER SPACE

Even if someday scientists were finally able to use their combined intelligence to create life from insentient materials, all that this will have, then, served to have proved is that life is even possible. But no one doubts that life is possible. We're here. In fact, the only people who still wonder if life is possible are those Woke thirty-somethings who are still living in their parents' basements.

The question isn't "can life exist" but rather "how did life first come to be?" and, after all of these years, the Materialists still don't have even the very first clue. Do you know who else didn't have even the very first clue? Whoever it was who came just before the world's second caveman.

Dawkins, the Oxford University professor, considered by many to be the single most effective spokesmodel for the Atheists' various origin myths, was once asked for his expert understanding as to how life might have first come into being without God.

Dawkins, who likes to be called an "evolutionary biologist" even though the chair for "propagandist" is in the history department, took a moment to compose himself and then, with that very same look of chagrin on his face that my friend Ed had had, he said that it was all just a "happy accident!"

"Happy accident" is not a scientific theory. It's how a fifty-year-old describes his newborn child through gritted teeth. In fact, not only is "happy accident" not a scientific theory; it is the very opposite of one. It is just yet one more way the professional Atheists have for saying "Duh, I dunno...shit happens."

We are now a full third of the way into the Big Questions upon which all of science itself is based, and while the Bible has given us the very laws and constants upon which all other science is contingent, the Atheists can still do nothing more than just point and grunt, albeit in Dawkins' case, with a relatively charming British accent.

It's not as if the Atheists don't have *any* other theories about the origin of life on earth besides "happy accident."

After ten thousand years, of course they do. They, in fact, have exactly one left that hasn't yet been totally debunked by that which is already known. The Atheists call their last remaining viable theory "Directed Panspermia."

The concept behind the theory of "directed panspermia" is that a horny drag queen from outer space came to earth on a transit beam and then...oh, wait. I'm sorry. That's *The Rocky Horror Picture Show*. In the Atheists' theory the horny space aliens came to earth on a *rocketship*.

Seriously, this is the Atheists' latest, best and, since "shit happens" isn't actually a theory, only remaining theory as to how life might have begun on Earth without God. According to the Atheists, the horny space aliens, then, somehow impregnated the planet and, in doing so, not only became earth's baby-daddies but also the universe's very first deadbeat dads.

While the notion of horny aliens from outer space having had sex with the earth is just as absurd as is the "Flying Spaghetti Monster" that Dawkins has cynically compared to the God of the Bible, the difference is that while Jews and Christians don't actually believe in the Flying Spaghetti Monster, the world's leading Atheistic "scientists" – including Dawkins – really do say that they believe in flying horndogs from outer space who, then, had sex with the earth.

If you think I'm kidding, here's Hargon's comments on Overbye's report:

> *The most startling revelation in Overbye's article is that scientists have resuscitated a proposal once floated by [Francis] Crick. Dissatisfied with conventional theories of life's beginning, Crick conjectured that aliens came to Earth in a spaceship and planted the seeds of life here billions of years ago.*

Crick is no crank. He is, in fact, the legendary geneticist who was awarded the Nobel Prize for co-discovering the DNA's double-helix design.

Crick didn't propose the Atheists' Flying-Horndogs-from-Outer-Space-Having-Had-Sex-With-The-Earth theory because he'd just seen a starship racing away at warp speed when Earth's husband returned home early from work, or because he'd suddenly discovered remnants of alien sperm on the arctic ice sheets. In fact, the only evidence that supports the Atheists' theory of horny aliens from outer space having had sex with the earth is the fact that the aliens haven't called once since.

Crick didn't propose FHFOS because there was any evidence for it; he proposed it wholly by default. Just as the Atheists' totally made-up their alternative universes and additional dimensions only after having concluded that there is simply nothing in ours that could possibly provide the Materialists with an answer that would allow them to keep their prior political commitment, Crick understood that there is simply nothing on earth a Materialist can use to possibly even begin to explain how life might have first come from the lifeless without God. Once again – and as always – when you're an Atheist, no evidence is always your best evidence, because all of the known evidence has fully debunked your every other effort.

Crick, then, only did what all good scientists do; he simply proposed the next, least implausible theory that hasn't yet been totally debunked by the known facts, which, at this point for the Atheists, is flying horndogs from outer space having had sex with the earth. That's it. That's all they have left.

When Crick first proposed FHFOS in 1973 it was, of course, rejected out-of-hand by the scientific community as the wholly unsubstantiated, patent absurdity that it is. A full half-century later, though – with the quantum leap forward in technological capabilities having only further confirmed that no materialistic answer can possibly ever be found on earth without God – Crick's theory of the Flying-Horndogs-from-Outer-Space-Having-Had-Sex-With-The-Earth is now the leading theory amongst Atheistic scientists. In fact, since "happy accident" isn't actually a theory, FHFOS is the *only* remaining theory that the Atheists have left for how life might have begun on earth without God.

Here's how Dawkins explains the "scientific" method that the Atheists use to arrive at their theory of FHFOS:

> *Given the weaknesses of all theories of terrestrial genesis, Directed Panspermia should be considered a serious possibility.*

That's it. That's the *entirety* of the evidence for the Atheists' only remaining theory as to how life might have begun on earth without God; all of their other theories are even worse. Not only is Atheistic "science" a joke; it's actually an old one:

> *This guy was just such a miserable human being in every conceivable way that when he died no one could think of even a single kind word to say about him at his funeral. Finally, one of his neighbors made his way to the altar, cleared his throat and said: "His brother was even worse."*

The entire "scientific" basis upon which the Atheists' current, best and only remaining theory as to how life might have begun on earth without God, is that all of their other theories are even worse. Even worse than horny space aliens having humped a flying rock? Just how bad must those other theories be? Well, we'll soon find out.

Meanwhile, with FHFOS having in no way advanced the scientific case for atheism, the Atheists have, once again, further made the case for God. Even when they're just totally making up stories wholly unconstrained by the need for such pesky things as evidence and reason, the Atheists *still* can't even conjure a tale that doesn't require preexisting life (the aliens) with, in this case, the intelligence to have designed rocket ships capable of intergalactic travel. You'd think, being that advanced, they'd have also have invented the condom.

Not to be missed, then, is that just as the Atheists have already conceded the most essential elements of the science of Intelligent Design with regard to the first of the Big Questions by admitting that the universe simply had to have been created by something or someone outside of our physical laws and/or perceivable dimensions, they have now conceded the most essential element of the second question as well. By their embrace of FHFOS, the Atheists have admitted that life could not have started on earth without a preexisting and intelligent lifeform from somewhere else.

Once again, then, both sides are in total agreement about what it is that the known science shows and where it that that science leads; the only difference is found in the fact that, while believers in the science of Intelligent Design and the revelations of the Bible are convinced that that preexisting intelligent life is from one of those universes and/or dimensions that the Atheists have already been forced to concede, the Atheists' combined efforts, cutting edge technology and many and massive computers has led them to conclude that it must have been a couple of horny aliens, cruising the galaxies in their rocket ship until they took sexual advantage of a planet they saw was looking a little blue. The entirety of the evidence for the Atheists' embrace of FHFOS is that all of their other theories are even worse.

CHAPTER FOUR

MAGIC SOUP AND COSMIC CRAPS

Whether the Atheists' claim is that life "somehow" began in outer space and then horny aliens planted their seed in the earth, or they cling to some or another failed terrestrial theory that life began on earth through some sort of act of immaculate conception (talk about ironic!), the professional Atheists' only theory with regard to anything thus far discussed or to follow is "luck."

Luck, of course, is not a scientific hypothesis. It's what people like Dawkins say when someone else wins the Nobel Prize again. In fact, not only is "luck" not a scientific hypothesis; it is the very opposite of one. It is just one more way the professional Atheists have for saying "duh, I dunno...shit happens!"

Since luck is all that the Atheists have, though, it behooves us to, at least, do our due diligence and try to look into the odds. Having been behooved, I behaved and I looked into them and, well, they're just not very good. Yeah, they're just not very good at all. In fact, if the Atheists' every theory wasn't already and in every known way scientifically impossible, they'd all, then, just be statistically impossible. After that, they'd all, then, just be patently absurd, wholly unsubstantiated, and extravagantly failed in their every test.

The odds of the universe having been so perfectly fine-tuned to even just first allow for the mere possibility of life having randomly created itself from the materials and forces in our universe were calculated by California Institute of Technology astrophysicist Herbert Ross:

> *The probability of all these known parameters randomly coming together would be one chance in ten to the two hundred eighty-second power, a probability so incredibly tiny that statistically speaking, it's impossible.*

That's one in ten with two hundred eight-two zeros after it. Think about it this way: one with three zeros after it is one in a thousand; six zeros is one in a million; nine zeros is one in a billion, twelve is one in a trillion and fifteen is one in a quadrillion. After that, there'd just be another 267 zeros to go.

Ross went on to explain:

Today we can measure the degree of fine-tuning design. For example, several of the constants of physics; we can show that they must be tuned to, say, better than one part in ten thousand trillion trillion trillion.

To put that number into perspective, there's a better chance of finding a U-Haul in California.

One in ten thousand trillion trillion trillion aren't the odds of the perfect universe having "somehow" "just happened" to have "somehow" "just happened." Those are the odds of just *one* of the constants of the universe having "somehow" "just happened" to have "somehow" "just happened."

To date, scientists know of over eight hundred such constants. More are still being discovered. The odds of the universe having so perfectly finetuned itself through the random interactions of insentient materials, then – if it wasn't already and in every and all known ways scientifically impossible – is about one in eighty million trillion trillion trillion. The only thing in the universe known to have that kind of luck is Miley Cyrus.

That's about how many "happy accidents" that would have had to have "somehow" "just happened" to have "somehow" "just happened" for just the creation of a universe so perfectly finetuned to then just even first begin to allow for the possibility of life. We haven't even yet begun to discuss the odds of that first life – let's call him "Fred" – having "somehow" "just happened" to have "somehow" "just happened" to have randomly have come from there.

According to the Atheists, first there would have had to have "somehow" "just happened" to have "somehow" "just happened" to have been "some sort" of Magic Soup. Just where this Magic Soup might have come from, the Atheists don't say. Nor do they say if it came with un-limited salad and breadsticks. The Atheists just say that it was just "somehow" there and that it just "somehow" "just happened" to cover the near entirety of the earth or what today would be about two-thirds of Alec Baldwin.

According to the Atheists, this magic soup that "some-how" "just happened" to have randomly appeared also "somehow" "just happened" to have "somehow" "just hap-pened" to have contained all of the right ingredients to have then "somehow" "just happened" to have produced a very specific set of chemical reactions.

Did I say a "very specific" set of chemical reactions? Make that a "very, very, very specific" set of chemical reactions. How specific? So specific that no scientist in the past ten thousand years has yet been able to recreate them.

These very, very, very specific chemical reactions, the Atheists say, then "somehow" "just happened" to have created amino acids which then "somehow" "just happened" to have created proteins which then "somehow" "just happened" to have combined to have, then, "somehow" "just happened" to have "somehow" "just happened" to have "somehow" created the "whatever" of life.

I keep saying "somehow", "in some way" and "whatever" not just because *I* don't know; I keep saying it because *they* don't know. The Atheists haven't even a clue. Not even the very first one. About any of it. Not even just one small part.

Meanwhile, not a single one of the things that the Atheists claim simply must have "somehow" "just happened" to have "somehow" "just happened" is based on any of the known laws or constants of any of the known fields of science nor are they substantiated by even a single observation, discovery or experiment – you know, what real scientists call "data." The Atheists simply made them all up in just the same way that they simply just made up the multiverse, dangling strings and horny aliens from outer space having had sex with the earth.

As one typically does, let's start with the soup. There is simply no evidence that the Atheists' Magic Soup ever existed. It remains a possibility that the aliens from

Panspermia ate it – after all, who *isn't* hungry after having just had sex with a planet? – but, given just how much of the earth the Atheists say this Magic Soup simply had to have "somehow" "just happened" to have "somehow" "just happened" to have covered, this lack of evidence alone should be damning. Unless, of course, you're a professional Atheist. Then a lack of evidence is the only thing that makes one of your theories still viable.

Even if the Atheists' claim is that the aliens took the Magic Soup to go, it would have still left a residue on the side of the "bowl" in just the same way that your minestrone soup leaves a residue on the side of your cup or your Uncle Frank leaves a residue whenever he gets up from the couch. Okay, maybe that's just *my* Uncle Frank.

No evidence of such residue has ever been found. Not even one drop. Not even one the size of Tom Cruise and, believe me, the Atheists have been searching. Frantically. Night and day. Across the globe. For years on end.

Once again, then, when you're an Atheist no evidence is always your best evidence. When it comes to those chemical reactions the Atheists say simply must have "somehow" "just happened" to have "somehow" "just happened" in the Magic Soup - well, we know what those chemicals were likely to have been on earth at the time and we also know that they don't react in the ways that the Atheists claim that they'd have had to have reacted in order for them to have, then, "somehow" "just happened" to have "somehow" "just happened" to have created the "whatever" of life.

In fact, what we know is that these chemicals often react in the very *opposite* way. As University of California, San Diego chemistry professor, Edward Peltzer, explains:

> *Random chemical reactions are both woefully insufficient and are often working against the pathways needed to succeed.*

"Often working against." Not only have the Atheists gotten nowhere since the very first day of the world's very first caveman, they're now actually going backwards.

Peltzer then added:

> *It is the very chemistry that speaks of a need for something more than just time and chance.*

Actually, as Overbye and Horgan make clear, it's the very chemistry, biology, physics, and astronomy along with every known law and constant of every other known field of science, as well as ten thousand years of literally every observation, discovery, and experiment – you know, what real scientists call "data" – that speaks of a need for something more than just time and chance.

The professional Atheists know this, too, by the way, which is why they've had to make up those other universes, dimensions, and planets where they promise that that "something more" has been hiding from them this whole time.

Peltzer then concluded by saying:

> *For these reasons I have serious doubts about whether the current paradigm will ever make additional progress.*

Considering the fact that the Atheists' "current paradigm" of time and chance (a.k.a. "Duh, I dunno…shit happens!") has thus far made *no* progress and hasn't, even once in the past ten thousand years, serious doubts about *additional* progress provides for easy calculation.

The exact formula was first proposed by the great 1970's mathematician and singing sensation Billy Preston who correctly postulated in a song that rose to Number One on the pop charts that "nothing from nothing leaves nothing."

Just as with the advent of the universe, when it comes to how life might have first come from the insentient without God, the Atheists start with nothing and after all of these years, the Atheists are left with nothing and, as far as I'm concerned, I agree with Dr. Preston Ph. D-minor, "you've got to have *something* if you want to be with me."

With no evidence of the Magic Soup and with every chemical reaction being not just woefully insufficient for, but often working against the Atheists' current (and only politically acceptable) paradigm of time and chance, the next process the Atheists claim simply must have then "somehow" "just happened" to have "somehow" "just happened" – the creation of the proteins that would have then had to have "somehow" "just happened" to have "somehow" "just happened" to have provided for the "whatever" of life – is just yet another scientific absurdity and statistical impossibility piled on top of all of the other scientific absurdities and statistical impossibilities that comprise the entirety of Atheistic "science" to date. That date, by the way, is denoted in scientific literature as ten thousand A.W.V.F.C. or After the World's Very First Caveman.

Surely you remember from your elementary school chemistry class – or, if you were born after 1980, your post-doctoral thesis – a protein is a chain of various amino acids of different shapes and sizes. The length of each chain along with which amino acids are in it creates each unique and very specific protein. Did I say "very specific" protein? Make that "very, very, very specific" protein.

If you change the length of the chain, you change the protein's function. If you change the amino acids in the chain, you change the protein's function. Scientists estimate that there were over 350 proteins in just Fred alone. Just one of these proteins – and a relatively small one at that – consists of over 150 very, very, very specific amino acids.

The odds of a chain with 150 variables and just those variables alone having come together through a series of random interactions of insentient materials requires scientists to use numbers so infinitesimal that I can't even pronounce them, while employing symbols so rarely used that I've never even seen them before.

However one pronounces the statistically impossible odds against 150 amino acids "somehow" "just happening" to come together, those odds, then, must not just be added to but multiplied by all of the other statistically impossible odds for each of the patently absurd, wholly unsubstantiated. and extravagantly failed other parts of the Atheists' origin myth. As it turns out, nothing *times* nothing is nothing, too.

As bad as the odds against the Atheists' origin myth are so far, they aren't even anywhere near as good as that.

That's because a particular protein not only needs just the right *number* of just the right *kind* of just the right very, very, very specific amino acids; but it also needs for them to all then "somehow" "just happen" to "somehow" "just happen" to all be in just the right *order*. If you move even one of the amino acids' positions in the chain, you change the protein's function.

What makes the odds of winning the Powerball jackpot so staggeringly unlikely is not merely that you have to rightly pick six numbers out of sixty-nine possibilities – already an incredibly long shot – but that the sixth number (the ball with the "power" to make you rich) has to come up in just the right order (last).

That one ball alone changes the odds against winning by orders of magnitude. Simply consider the difference in the meager payout for getting five numbers right and the massive payoff for getting the sixth number as well.

Actually, the odds still wouldn't be even anywhere near *that* good for the Atheists, because proteins aren't just a two-dimensional chain; they're a three-dimensional shape. Proteins need to "fold over" onto themselves in order to, then, perform their functions.

These folds can happen anywhere along the chain. The odds that any one of these proteins would "just happen" to "somehow" "just happen" to fold over at just the right spot along those 150 amino acids in the chain are, well, statistically impossible.

And things only just keep getting worse for the Atheists from here. Many of the proteins essential for life require *multiple* folds. These folds all then need to not only "somehow" "just happen" to "somehow" "just happen" at just the right spot along the chain; they all need to "somehow" "just happen" to "somehow" "just happen" all in just the right order.

At this point in the Atheists' second least-worst theory, if every single one of these things had "somehow" "just happened" and they all "somehow" "just happened" just-so (and all in the right order) the universe would have had it's very first protein. Now, there are only another 349 more to go.

Oh, and how do the Atheists say these randomly created proteins – like teeny-weenie Lego pieces in a giant bowl of Magic Soup – came together to form Fred? They say they just "somehow" "just happened" to have "somehow" "just happened" to have "somehow" assembled themselves. All 350 of them. All in just the right order.

Meanwhile, this isn't even the Atheists' theory about how life began on earth. This is simply their least worst terrestrial theory about what would have had to have "somehow" "just happened" to have "somehow" "just happened" just to have created the *materials* – the proteins – that would have, then, still have had to have "somehow" "just happened" to have "somehow" "just happened" to have, then, come to life.

So, what is the Atheists' least worst terrestrial theory as to how the insentient proteins that "somehow" "just happened" to have made Fred come to life? It depends on where you are. Where the Atheists speak Samoan, they say "Duh, ou te le iloa ... o mea leaga e tupu." Where the Atheists speak Esperanto, they say "Duh, mi ne scias... feko okazas." Wherever the Atheists speak English, though, they just say

"Duh, I dunno...shit happens."

CHAPTER FIVE

ROCKY, UGG! DR. LEWONTIN, UGG!

For the Atheists, their problems are only just beginning. This is because, according to the Atheists' second least-worst theory, after all of these scientifically and statistically impossible things all "somehow" "just happened" to have "somehow" "just happened", all that we'd have is Fred, the very first simple lifeform.

The problem is that, when scientists – real scientists – say "simple" they mean it only in comparison to the more complex lifeforms that God (or luck) later created. The reality is that, whatever form that first lifeform took, it couldn't have possibly been all that simple. In fact, just for Fred to have survived, he'd have had to have "somehow" "just happened" to have "somehow" "just happened" to have been rather complex.

When I say "complex," I don't mean it in the way that Billie Eilish is "complex." That's the last thing the universe would have needed at that moment; a suicidal first life. I mean, that in order to have survived, Fred would have needed to have been *structurally* complex.

For one thing, Fred would have needed to have been able to create the energy to operate. Since there was nothing else yet living – no plants or animals for him to eat – Fred would have been in trouble. Luckily, having no brain made Fred a vegan, and so the Atheists say he just "somehow" synthesized light from the sun.

Talk about luck! No other set of Legos in the known universe comes with even double A batteries included, but according to the Atheists, Fred "somehow" "just happened" to have "somehow" "just happened" to have randomly arisen from the dead with his own state-of-the-art solar energizer pack.

When I say "state-of-the-art," I don't mean the state of the art then, either; I mean the state of the art *now*! The Atheists' second least-worst theory about how life might have begun on earth without God is that billions of years of random luck "somehow" "just happened" to have "somehow" "just happened" to have provided Fred with better solar panels then we have today. Who knows, maybe the Atheists' claim is that Fred's last name was Musk.

But that's not all! In addition to luck having "somehow" "just happened" to have "somehow" "just happened" to have created the universe's first and only box of self-assembling and self-energizing Legos, the Atheists say that a few more trillion trillion (trillion trillion) "happy accidents" "somehow" "just happened" to have "somehow" "just happened" to have made Fred self-propelling.

Yup, the Atheists say that Fred was able to scoot around faster than Amber Heard running off of the witness stand because, as luck would have it, Fred "somehow" "just happened" to have "somehow" "just happened" to have come with his own built-in outboard motor.

But wait, there's more! According to the Atheists, not only were these Legos "somehow" self-assembling, self-energizing and self-propelling but, if you call now, the Atheists will *double* your order because Fred, they say, "somehow" "just happened" to have "somehow" "just happened" to have "somehow" come to life capable of self-replication!

That's right, the Atheists say that Fred "somehow" "just happened" to have crawled out of the Magic Soup with the ability to recreate his innards, double his outards and split in half to become two in a process many fear Whoopi Goldberg is attempting to recreate today.

Well, there you have it, folks. After ten thousand years, it's the Atheists' latest, best and, in fact, only remaining terrestrial theory about how life might have come from the insentient without God and it is so patent an absurdity that not even the Atheists themselves believe it. In fact, today, the world's leading Atheistic "scientists" from across the globe, working night and day, with cutting edge technologies and high-speed computers, have crunched the data and concluded that there's a better chance that life started on earth when a horny alien schtupped a flying rock.

Of course, the Atheists don't actually *call* it "Magic Soup." Even they know that that would make them look ridiculous and so, to make themselves appear at least somewhat serious, they call it the more scientificky-sounding "Primordial Ooze." And, of course, the Atheists don't call them "self-assembling Legos." Even they know that would make them look like fools, so to make the ludicrous appear, well, at least somewhat less ludicrous, they call them the "Building Blocks" that they say then "somehow" "just happened" to have "somehow" "just happened" to have "somehow" assembled themselves.

As for the Atheists saying that their entire origin myth is based on nothing more than the nonscientific concept of "luck," well, they prefer to not just come right out and say it. Instead, they call the whole process the "Cosmic

Lottery." Of course, even the lottery requires preexisting life with the intelligence to have put the game together.

They do, though. They really, really do describe their entire theory about anything and everything in the universe as the "Cosmic Lottery." Luck, however, is not a scientific theory. The Atheists simply don't have one. About the origin of anything. Anywhere. Ever. There is simply nothing in the laws of our sciences or the forces and materials in our universe that even allow the Atheists just to conjure a theory about anything without God.

In fairness, not every Atheistic scientist who attempts to sell the Materialists' political doctrine compares their every effort to such nonscientific random games of luck as the lottery. Others prefer to compare them to the nonscientific random games of luck known as "craps" and "roulette."

This is how Stephen Hawking, considered by many to have been the greatest theoretical physicist of our time – emphasis on the word "theoretical" – describes the basis of all Atheistic theory in his book *Brief Answers to the Big Questions*:

> *The Universe is like a giant casino, with dice being rolled, or wheels being spun on every occasion.*

It's hard to argue with someone who is said to have been as brilliant as Dr. Hawking, but there does appear to be at least one small problem with his claim: it's patently absurd. The universe isn't random.

In fact, if the universe were random, there'd be no such thing as science. This is why there is no actual science – none of the known laws or constants of any of the known sciences nor a single observation, discovery or experiment – to be found anywhere in any of the Atheists' various theories about the Big Questions.

The very definition of science – "the systemically organized body of knowledge on a particular subject" – is the very opposite of randomness. There is no "system", there is no "organization", and there is no "knowledge" to randomness. Simply, to prove a theory to be right requires the ability to predict outcomes. If the universe were random, we would no more be able to predict the outcome of various interactions than one can predict the outcome of the lottery.

But we can and we do predict outcomes all the time. We can predict that, unless otherwise acted upon, an apple will fall *down* from a tree. We can predict that a planet will orbit in an *elliptical* fashion. My God, even Annie, a six-year-old little orphan child, knew that the sun was going to come out tomorrow, but the Atheists claim that it's a longshot?

So, what's really going on? Why does even someone as highly-respected as Stephen Hawking swear to something so absurd that even a penniless orphan would bet her bottom dollar against it? Well, Lewontin has already provided the answer. The Atheists are so committed to their political doctrine that they swear by even the most patently absurd, wholly unsubstantiated, and extravagantly failed nonsense stories because otherwise they'd be admitting to design. In order to keep their "prior commitment" to Atheism, the Atheists must deny the existence of not just God, but of science as well.

CHAPTER SIX

MONKEY SEE, MONKEY DO, MONKEY TYPE?

Contrary to the image most of us have in our heads, when professional Atheist "scientists" go to work each day, they don't use their time to attempt to seek out the answers to any of the Big Questions. They already know the answers they're committed to giving, no matter what the science may actually, then, show.

Instead, the professional Atheists spend their entire day – in fact, their entire careers – desperately searching for just one thing and one thing only: the very first clue from even just any one of the various fields of science that might, at least in some way, merely even first begin to just possibly suggest that even just one part of even just one of their theories might even be possible. Not that any of it actually happened, mind you, just that even one small part of the Atheists' origin myth is even possible. Thus far, after ten thousand years, the Atheists have utterly failed in their every attempt.

In the meantime, unable to point to even a single law or provide even just a lone observation, discovery, or experiment – you know, what real scientists call "data" – that suggests that any part of their origin myth is even possible, the Atheists have been forced to resort to an antiscientific rhetorical gimmick whereby they claim only that their theories haven't been proved to be *impossible*. Of course, that might just be because it's impossible to prove that something's impossible. At least I think it is. How does one even go about trying to prove that horny aliens from outer space *didn't* have sex with the earth?

This rhetorical gimmick is so oft-used by the Atheists and, thus, it is so well-known, that it actually has a name. It's called the "Infinite Monkey" theorem and chances are that you've heard the professional Atheists say it - something like this:

> *If you put enough monkeys in a room with enough type-writers for enough time, eventually they'll type the collective works of William Shakespeare.*

Now, in fairness, there are some Materialists who recognize that no one is going to actually believe that all of those monkeys could have possibly fit into a single room, and so they attempt to make their theory sound just a little less implausible by claiming that the monkeys did their typing in outer space.

Either way, whether the Atheists' claim is that the monkeys were all in one giant room on earth or that they did their work while orbiting the globe, the Atheists' point remains the same: the Atheists' various origin theories aren't each, and all, and in every way impossible because, with enough time, *anything's* possible.

"Anything's possible" is not a scientific theory. It's what a petulant child says when his mother asks him if the cookies just all ate themselves. In fact, not only is "anything's possible" not a scientific theory; it is just another way the professional Atheists have for denying the existence of science.

Stick with me, I could be wrong here, but I'm fairly sure that the very reason that we call them the *laws* of science is because they're laws that can't be broken. Not even after a really, really, really long time. I'm pretty confident that the very reason that we call them the *constants* of science is because they're constant. There can simply *never* be "enough" time for a constant to not be constant for the simple reason that it's constant. Oy vey! ("Duh" just wouldn't have cut it.) If just anything is possible, then there simply are no laws or constants of science.

Atheistic "science," then, is so totally devoid of any actual science that just to simply attempt to make the case that even one small part of even just one of their patently absurd and both scientifically and statistically impossible theories about even just one small part of even just one of the Big Questions isn't impossible – not that it actually happened; just that it's not impossible for it to happen – the Atheists must deny the existence of science.

This, of course, shouldn't be surprising since a monotheistic God is the first and only requisite for the existence of science. If one has a prior commitment to denying the existence of God, then they also have a prior commitment to denying the existence of science.

Ironically (or perhaps just tellingly), there's a word in the English language that's defined as "'happy accidents' that cannot be explained by the laws and constants of science." That word is "miracle":

mir·a·cle

[ˈmirək(ə)l]

NOUN

1. a surprising and welcome event that is not explicable by natural or scientific laws and is therefore considered to be the work of a divine agency.

With the Atheists having already conceded to the believers that the universe had to have come from outside of our physical laws and perceivable dimensions, that life on earth couldn't possibly have started without a preexisting and intelligent life from somewhere beyond our planet and that, by attempting to conduct science, that the things in the universe have design, and that by invoking the Infinite Monkey theorem, the Atheists have now conceded that, for even any one part of even just one of their theories to not be impossible, it would take a miracle.

Meanwhile even when they're just making up patently absurd, antiscientific, rhetorical gimmicks like monkeys with typewriters in outer space, the Atheists are once again reaffirming the basic tenets of Intelligent Design and the Bible. Even the Atheists' Infinite Monkey theorem requires preexisting life (the monkeys), with the intelligence, in this case, to have invented the typewriter.

Oh, and one last thing about the Atheists' Infinite Monkey theorem. It's not even theoretically true. No matter how many monkeys you put in a room with any number of typewriters, all you'd end up with in no time at all, is a whole bunch of smashed typewriters and shredded papers with blood and feces covering the walls or, as we used to call it when I worked in Hollywood, "The Writer's Room."

SCIENCE, MARTY? WHERE WE'RE GOING, WE DON'T NEED SCIENCE

Clearly, when just to attempt to make the case that their theories aren't in each, and all, and in every part scientifically impossible, the Atheists must cite primates composing Elizabethan poetry in outer space, there's not a whole lot of science behind their efforts.

So how is it, then, that so many people still think of the Atheists as "The Scientists," while seeing those of us who are skeptical about typing monkeys in outer space, flying horndogs who had sex with a rock, and Magic Soup that creates self-replicating and self-assembling Legos as the "antiscientific whackos?"

The answer is that, when it comes to dealing with the Big Questions, the Atheists have simply changed the definition of "science" to service their political commitment and, in having done so, they've had to do nothing less than totally reverse the very method by which post-Enlightenment science is conducted. This is why Lewontin could say with a straight face that the professional Atheists "take the side of science," even as he then flatly admits to their engaging in its systematic and ritual betrayal.

Most people think that the Scientific Method was created to keep religious beliefs out of science. It was and it wasn't. It was created to keep *all* "prior commitments" including, yes, religious beliefs, but also things like cultural biases, personal ambitions, financial interests, and political doctrines like Militant Atheism, out of scientific *calculations*.

The Scientific Method, however, says nothing at all about scientific *conclusions*. In fact, the only thing that the Scientific Method says about what one may or may not conclude is that *nothing* is to be preordained and *nothing* is to be precluded if that's where following the method's protocols lead.

These protocols are really rather simple and straightforward: at its most basic, scientists are to work from left to right – from data collection and its analysis to conclusion – including in that data only that which has been collected through careful observation, discovery, and experiment.

At the same time, the analysis of that data must be made using only the known laws and constants of this universe and in only these four dimensions within which we humans can perceive. Things outside of this universe or these dimensions can absolutely be considered as the *conclusion* – the Atheists have already conceded this with their own theories about multiple universes and additional dimensions – they simply cannot be used in the *calculations*.

When it comes to the Big Questions, the Atheists have totally reversed this process. The Atheists work from right to left, with a materialistic conclusion preordained and immovable by the data. Just which materialistic answer the Atheists might choose to go with at any given time – the Flying Horndogs from Outer Space or the Magic Soup and self-replating Legos for example – might still be under discussion, but the Atheists have committed themselves ahead of time to a conclusion that serves their political agenda, no matter what the actual data and its analysis may show.

Since all known data supports the God hypothesis, the Atheists must simply ignore all of the known facts and since all of the known laws and constants from every known field of science makes clear that their preor-dained and politically-motivated conclusions aren't even possible, the Atheists must simply deny that the laws and constants of science exist.

Clearly, then, the Atheists aren't called "The Scientists" because there is any actual science on either side of their scientific ledger: calculations or conclusions. There is literally none on either side. The Atheists are only called "The Scientists" because they've completed their betrayal of the Scientific Method by precluding the only other possible scientific alternative.

Since there are only two possibilities – either there's a creator and the universe was designed or there's no creator and everything is luck – and in violation of the protocols of the Scientific Method, the professional Atheists have precluded one of them, the Atheists are only called "The Scientists" because they've left us with no other choice.

The Atheists have simply redefined "Science" to mean the political doctrine of "Materialism," no matter how totally and in every conceivable way it fails as a scientific theory. The Atheists' problem is that, since a monotheistic God is the one and only requisite for the existence of science, by precluding that God from their conclusions, the Atheists are forced to exclude all science from their calculations.

By reversing the Scientific Method, the Atheists have returned to the pre-Enlightenment days when doctrine – religious then, political now – determines what the powers-that-be will allow to be called "The Science." By rejecting every observation, discovery, and experiment – you know, what real scientists call "data" – from over the course of the past ten thousand years, the Atheists have returned to the very first day of the world's very first caveman, back before the very first observation, discovery. or experiment had ever even taken place. Ugg, indeed!

CHAPTER EIGHT

YOUR TESTS HAVE COME BACK NEGATIVE AGAIN, DR. LEWONTIN

When a scientist proposes a theory, that theory makes certain predictions. These are the "promises" that Lewontin referred to in his confession. The Scientific Method then demands that, if these predictions are significantly and repeatedly proved right through observation, discovery, and experiment – you know, what real scientists call "data" – then that theory must be embraced by the scientific community as a whole, without regard to whatever the religious, financial, professional, or political ramifications might be.

If, on the other hand, these predictions are clearly and repeatedly proved by the data to have been wrong, then the Scientific Method demands that that theory must be discarded, also without regard to the potential religious, financial, professional, or political consequences.

Over the course of the past ten thousand years – ever since the world's very first caveman made his very first observation – there has not ever, even once, been a single prediction an Atheist "scientist" has made about any of the Big Questions that hasn't not only clearly, repeatedly, and in every conceivable way been proved by the data to have been wrong, but that hasn't been proved by the data to have been anything other than the very opposite of right. This is what Lewontin meant by the Atheists' promises being *extravagant* in their failures, and it is why the professional Atheists still haven't even the very first clue about even one small part of even just one of the Big Questions about creation and design.

The reason for the extravagance of the Atheists' failures is a tad complicated, but I'll attempt to explain the science here. Any theory like those of the Atheists that is based on the concept of randomness predicts a high degree of what scientists call "randomness." I'll wait while you do the calculations.

What all observation, discovery, and experiment – you know, what real scientists call "data" – show. is a stunning (some might even say "otherworldly") degree of precision. The Atheists have been wrong about everything and wrong to the Nth degree each and every time because precision is the precise opposite of randomness. Duh!

For example, it might be possible (you know, if it wasn't impossible) for the cosmos to have randomly finetuned itself to within one in eighty million trillion trillion trillion parts by "happy accident," but I think that we can at least all agree that that's not what the Atheist hypothesis predicts. In fact, it would literally be the Atheists' eighty million trillion trillion trillionth guess. The Scientific Method suggests that, if by, say, the seventy-nine million trillion trillion trillionth guess you still haven't gotten it right even once, it might just be time to consider the only other scientific alternative.

Meanwhile, such otherworldly precision is exactly what that only other scientific alternative predicts and it does so on its very first try. Did I say its "very first" try? Make that its "very, very, very first" try.

The Atheists' claim that the universe is random is so patent an absurdity that it's likely that the world's very first caveman knew it even before his first full week on earth was out. Surely by then he'd have said to himself "Fireball in sky start there, go there again. Ugg!"

This puts the caveman not just neck-and-neck with but way ahead of the professional Atheists with whom he is tied in every other way. After all, neither the caveman nor the Atheist had even the first clue as to *how* things happened, but both are equally well aware of the fact that that shit happens.

The difference, then, is only in that, unlike the Atheists, when the caveman discovered that shit happens, he likely didn't just point and grunt "luck." Instead, he'd surely already have concluded what Peltzer is only now discovering some ten thousand years later – the same thing the Atheists admit to when they make up other universes, dimensions, planets, and monkeys typing in outer space – "there has to be something more."

Being a better scientist than is the Atheist, the caveman, then, analyzed the data available to him at the time, and then postulated theories about how the things in the universe might work. Yes, of course the caveman's theories were primitive – he was a primitive for God's sake. Unlike today's scientists, he didn't have a whole lot of shoulders to stand on and, according to the drawings at least, those that he did have were hunched over and so he'd have only just kept falling off.

Still, I'm not sure that a caveman believing something as patently absurd as, say, "the sun is dragged across the sky on the backs of God's invisible turtles" is really all that much more primitive than is believing that life began on earth when flying horndogs from outer space slipped the big one to a giant rock.

In fact, from just a purely scientific standpoint, the caveman's theory is a much sounder theory than is the Atheists'. After all, unlike the horny aliens from outer space, at least we know that turtles actually exist.

Think about that! The caveman's very first theory, as patently absurd as it may have been, had more substantiation to it than anything an Atheist has proposed in the ten thousand years since. Of course, that's what happens when you base your entire theory on the movie *The Rocky Horror Picture Show*. In fact, you should see the dance the Atheists do when they're trying to prove the existence of a time warp.

As time went on and man learned more, the hypotheses postulated by the scientists of their times became more and more sophisticated and they went from "Ugg!" to things that we would later call "folklore," "legends" and "myths." Then one day, about three thousand years ago, a guy named Moses postulated a new theory of the universe.

Over the course of the next three millennia, as man has learned more and more through observation, discovery, and experiment – you know, what real scientists call "data" – what we've found at every turn has only more and more confirmed the predictions that Moses' theory makes. Einstein is only amongst one of the more recent scientists whose works have done just that.

In fact, even when the Atheists are required by their political doctrine to reject Moses' theory, their attempts to counter it with a theory of their own only sees them forced each and every time to reconfirm its most basic tenets and to move ever closer to it in its specifics.

Just how scientifically accurate the predictions made by Moses' theory have proved to have been was the subject of an interview in the *New York Times* – the *NEW YORK TIMES!!!* – conducted with the Nobel Prize-winning physicist, Arno Penzias:

> *The best data we have are exactly what I would have predicted had I had nothing to go on but the five books of Moses, the Psalms, the Bible as a whole.*

Three thousand years after Moses first postulated his theory, it remains the very basis of science itself. In fact, there could be no such thing as science without it. This is why there is no science to be found in those whose politics require them to deny it.

Meanwhile, if one were to simply apply just the most basic protocols of the Scientific Method to the Atheists' theory, Atheism would have been discarded some 9,999 years and 358 days ago at exactly 6:17 a.m., when the world's very first caveman saw that same one fireball rise yet again in the East and said, "The universe *isn't* random...Ugg!"

As bad as things are for the Atheist origin myth to this point; they only get worse for the Atheists from here.

CHAPTER NINE

NO INTELLIGENCE? SPEAK FOR YOURSELF

Imagine you're visiting the Grand Teton national park. You come up over a ridge and there, spelled out in pinecones, is a personalized welcome. It starts with regards to you and your wife, as well as your twins Melissa and Melvon (rightly spelled with an "o").

You continue to read and more and more precise details emerge including an offer to give you a ride back to your home at 8643 Constitution Blvd in Key Biscayne, Florida, (unit 4B) as well as both your landline and your cellphone numbers, area codes and all.

As more of the valley comes into view, it becomes obvious that the missive continues on for as far as the eye can see. It now lists the exact make, model and year of your car, your VIN, license plate and driver's license numbers, as well as the color of your eyes, your weight (your real one, not the one you put on your driver's license which you swore you'd be down to by now), and it even reminds you that your "check engine" light is on and why.

At this point, you might not know just *who* laid the pinecones out in this fashion or *why* they might have done such a thing, but if you then turned to a park ranger and asked him and he shrugged his shoulders and said, "Duh, I dunno...shit happens!" you'd likely seek out a better explanation. If he said, "monkeys in rooms with typewriters," you'd probably slug him for insulting your intelligence.

Yet this is exactly what the professional Atheists want you believe with regard to DNA and the far more massive, detailed, and precise information packed into the astounding computer code found in every living thing.

DNA doesn't just *resemble* computer code; DNA *is* computer code. Here's Dawkins' description:

> *DNA doesn't just resemble computer code; DNA is computer code.*

Dawkins elaborated in his book, *River Out of Eden*:

> *Apart from differences in jargon, the pages of a molecular biology journal might be interchanged with those of a computer engineering journal.*

When it comes to the fourth of the Big Questions – where the coding and machinery that runs every aspect of the cell (and, in turn the body) might have come from – once again, the Atheist can still only just point and grunt.

For the Atheists, it's the same old problems as always. There is simply no known law or laws of any of the known sciences that allows for information to come from non-intelligent sources, nor has there ever, even once, been a single observation, discovery, or experiment – you know, what real scientists call "data" – over the course of the past ten thousand years, that doesn't make clear that's it just simply scientifically impossible.

As far as we know, a rock has still never composed a poem – not even a simple haiku! – by all known observation, a planet is yet to have penned a single screenplay and, with the exception of Keith Richards, a fossil has still never been known to have written even just a song.

While it is wholly conceivable that monkeys with type-writers could repeatedly tap out a Jimmy Kimmel mono-logue, DNA actually contains enough specific code in but a single two-inch strand to have produced not just the collective works of Shakespeare, but every book, play, movie, TV show, record album, videogame, and com-puter program ever written. Combined. And then some. And then by orders of magnitude more. And that's in just a two-inch strand. The human DNA (when unfurled) is over six feet in length. DNA has two strands. In every one of the 37,000,000,000,000 different cells – of many types –that adult humans have in our body at any given time.

Consider the fact that just one four-letter word – "Help!" – written in the sand on an island thought to have been deserted, would serve as proof positive that an intelligent life had created it; but the Atheists' claim is that the equivalent of every human communication ever written in any form and in any medium inside of a two-inch strand of computer code, proves nothing at all about the existence of a creator. At this point I'm guessing that, if those horny aliens from outer space had known that some of their children would turn out to be this stupid, they'd have never have had sex with that giant rock in the first place.

Just how complex, precise and simply downright brilliant the DNA code is was only hinted at by Chris Williams, Ph.D., Biochemistry at the Ohio State University. He wrote:

Each of us has a vast 'computer program' of six billion DNA bases in every cell that guided our development from a fertilized egg, specifies how to make more than 200 tissue types, and ties all this together in numerous highly functional organ systems. Few people outside of genetics or biochemistry realize that scientists still can provide no substantive details at all about the origin of life, and particularly the origin of genetic information in the first self-replicating organism.

Allow me to repeat, as with literally every other Atheistic theory about anything and everything thus far discussed or to be discussed below, the Atheists can provide "no substantive details at all." As in none at all. As in *none at all*. At this point even the world's very first caveman would be saying "Hold my gruel!"

Things only get worse for the Atheists from here, because DNA is nothing more than a repository for information. It then needs someone or something to read it. Without a reader, the code would be like a CD without a CD player, a DVD without a DVD player, or a book in the hands of a public-school graduate in any major American city today.

The first thing that the cell's machinery must be able to do is to translate the complex computer code contained in the DNA strands. This alone is an incredibly daunting task. I sometimes can't even translate what Bernie Sanders is trying to say, and English is an infinitely simpler language.

Once translated, the machine then needs to *effectuate* the instructions; it must turn the code into action. The CD player, for example, must translate the code on the disc, turn it into sound and then play that sound for the listener. There is no actual music on a CD – and that's *any* CD and not just rap.

Next, with the code having "somehow" having been written and the machinery to translate and then effectuate it having "somehow" "just happened" to have come into existence, there then still needs for there to "somehow" "just happen" to "somehow" "just happen" to be the materials for the machinery to then act upon.

On an auto assembly line, for example, there first needs to be a robotic arm, and then there needs to be the code that tells it what to do, as well as the operating system to translate that code and command the arm into action.

At the same time, all of this would be for naught, if there isn't also a *car* on the assembly line that requires just that one specific task to be performed. Perhaps we're talking about a single bolt that then needs to be tightened, using just the right tool and just the right torque for just the exactly right amount of time.

That's for just one bolt. On just one car. Now consider the process with something as complex and precise as the human being and its six billion DNA bases in just a single cell.

Just a small part of what takes place on this "assembly line" in our cells was described in a recent article in *ScienceAlert*:

> *Inside every cell of the human body is a constellation of proteins, millions of them. They're all jostling about, being speedily assembled, folded, packaged, shipped, cut and recycled in a hive of activity that works at a feverish pace to keep us alive and ticking.*

Wow, right? I mean, that's even more than a worker at an Amazon warehouse does. Of course, in fairness, the cell probably gets paid more. Still, we know where Amazon came from; it was designed and created by a preexisting intelligent lifeform known as Jeff Bezos.

So where do the Atheists say that the DNA code, the operating system to translate and effectuate it and the materials for them to then act upon came from? Actually, it depends on where you are. Afrikaner Atheists say "Duh, ek dunno…kak gebeur." Estonian Atheists say "Duh, ma dunno…sitt juhtub." Dawkins, Lewontin and the other Atheists who speak English say: "Duh, I dunno…shit happens!"

Meanwhile, all I know is, if I'm ever stranded on a desert island, I pray to God it's not an Atheist who flies over.

CHAPTER TEN

WHO YOU GONNA BELIEVE A MILITANT ATHEIST OR YOUR LYING EYES?

For all of the patent absurdities, extravagantly failed promises, unsubstantiated just-so stories, and scientific and statistical impossibilities that atheism requires you to believe at each and every step of the way, there's one thing that the Militants desperately don't want you to believe: your eyes.

It is simply impossible to look around and not see the very precise, intricate, and purposeful design in literally everything in the universe, big and small – on earth and in the heavens – with the possible exception of season five of *The Marvelous Mrs. Maisel*. That was just an ungodly mess.

Not even the professional Atheists themselves deny that the coding and machinery of the DNA, the finetuning of the cosmos, and the structures of the body (for example) all look like they've been designed and created; they simply claim that it's all just a series of what Dawkins calls utterly "ingenious illusions."

Putting aside the fact that ingeniousness and randomness are opposites (duh!), there is simply no evidence that even suggests that what so clearly appears to have been designed wasn't designed. Of course, when you're an Atheist, no evidence is always your best evidence.

Once again, then, the Atheists and the believers are in total agreement about what the known science shows. We both agree that, by all appearances, the universe and everything in it seems to have been designed and created. The only difference is found in the fact that, while believers in both the science of Intelligent Design in general and the revelations of the Bible in particular, believe that the overwhelming appearance of intelligent design serves as a strong indicator of intelligent design; the Atheists just once again stomp their feet and screech, "luck!!!"

Luck, of course, is not a scientific hypothesis – it is, in fact, the very opposite of one. In fact, not only does Dawkins' wholly unsubstantiated proclamation do nothing to advance the Atheists' cause, it only serves to set them back even further.

Now, not only would "luck" have had to have "somehow" "just happened" to a have created the *mechanically* perfect universe; it would have also have had to have "somehow" "just happened" to have created one that *looks* so perfect, that its managed to fool virtually everyone who has ever lived.

Meanwhile, even if Dawkins' baseless proclamation were true, it wouldn't in any way provide a reason to doubt God's existence. In fact, it might even strengthen it.

I've worked in show business for almost my entire adult life. Show business is a profession where we create illusions on a daily basis. When you think that we've designed a working kitchen or a fully-functioning living room for a sit-com, it is only the illusion that those things were created. It still took a preexisting intelligent life – or at least a couple of Teamsters – to build them.

Think about it this way. The fact that Penn and Teller's Las Vegas show is filled with ingenious illusions does nothing to disprove the fact that Penn and Teller exist. Neither, by the way, does it in any way suggest that they suddenly came to life when they crawled out of the "primordial ooze" that describes any hotel pool in Nevada.

In fact, not only do Penn and Teller's illusions fail to disprove the existence of the magicians, it's the illusions themselves that helps to prove that Penn and Teller *are* magicians. Without those illusions, those two people over there could be just any portly guy with a beard and his short friend, or maybe even just Amy Schumer with some kid. The existence of the illusions is specifically what proves that Penn and Teller *are* magicians.

In fact, one might even conclude that, given the fact that their illusions have so successfully fooled so many smart people for so many years, the illusions Penn and Teller designed and created might make them even greater magicians than if the illusions had simply just happened by chance.

If all of the greatest magicians from across the globe and from throughout the whole of time were to, then, be invited backstage after the show and allowed to examine – and even reverse engineer – the illusions, using the most advanced and carefully calibrated array of equipment, and they all came out saying things like "luck," "happy accident," and "Duh, I dunno...shit happens," I think it would be fair to conclude that Penn and Teller might just be the greatest illusionists the world has ever known.

Like all theories, the Atheists' "Ingenious Illusions" gambit makes certain predictions that can be tested. For example, if we were to walk into the Penn and Teller theater one night before the show and see illusions set up on the stage, it would serve as a fairly good indicator to most that someone or something had designed and created those illusions. Duh!

It would also predict with near certainty that there are magicians somewhere nearby who have or will soon perform those illusions. Double Duh!

In fact, the mere existence of these illusions would predict something else and, once again and as always, it is the very opposite of what the Atheist hypothesis predicts. The existence of these illusions predicts that at some point there will likely be an *audience* there to see the show. Double Duh and then one more!

Yup, it's the rare *triple* duh. It's the hat-trick of duh. It's the trifecta of duh. One more "duh" and we'd have the theme song from the TV show *Dragnet*. (Duh-duh-duh-duh!). "Duh", of course, is the very opposite of the Atheists' each and every "patent absurdity" of which, even by their own admission, the Atheists have nothing other. About anything. Big or small. Anywhere on earth or in the entire universe. This universe or any of the others the Atheists have been forced to simply make up after all of their other theories have so extravagantly failed.

In fact, the Atheists' Ingenious Illusions gambit is even more precise in its predictions. The existence of these illusions would suggest that not only will there be an audience there to see the show, but it predicts just exactly who will be in that audience.

Canine, feline, bovine, and porcine wouldn't do. Life isn't a Cardi B. concert. Penn and Teller's audience would simply have to be comprised of beings capable of understanding and appreciating the show. The same would obviously be true no matter who or what created the illusions. Duh-duh-duh-duh-duuuuuh!

This, then, finally brings us to the most important question of all. It is a question of such singular import that it may well be the very first question a sentient human being ever asked. It is a question of such unparalleled significance that, for millennia, millions upon millions of people – many of them amongst the greatest minds of all time, including the vast majority of history's most brilliant scientists – have devoted their entire lives to trying to find the answer. Seeking its answer is, in fact, so instinctively a part of being human that it is the very first question that the purest of all scientists, the two-year-old child, asks (and asks, and asks, and asks), and that is "Why?"

Proving motive is an essential element in any prosecution; it seems to me, then, that it should be just as essential when prosecuting the laws of science. What reason could the universe have possibly have had to have created such ingenious illusions?

The Atheists, of course, can't even begin to answer this first and most essential of all human questions. Like an episode of *The View*, as soon as reason is introduced to an Atheist, the conversation ends. The reason for this is simple: randomness and reason are opposites.

Those who embrace the science of Intelligent Design in general, however, can answer the question of "why?" in general: it's because the designer wanted it that way. Believers in the revelations of the Bible specifically, can answer the question specifically, and they can do so based on all known observation, discovery, and experiment – you know, what real scientists call "data" – from throughout the entire course of all of human experience. The only reason that the universe would have created the illusion of design is to thrill and amaze, awe and delight an audience. And not just any audience; one that is capable of understanding and appreciating the show.

And, wouldn't you know it, by yet one more scientifically and statistically impossible four-billion-year long game of "Cosmic Craps," here we are. And we *are* thrilled and amazed, awed, and delighted. In fact, even someone as dark and devious as Dawkins has been known to crack a smile every now and then. Now what are the odds of *that*!

CHAPTER ELEVEN

WELL, I'LL BE A MONKEY'S NON-GENDER SPECIFIC RELATIVE

Finally, about ten billion years into the Atheists' patently absurd, wholly unsubstantiated, and always and in every way failed politically-motivated origin myth – right at its very, very, very end, in fact– we're introduced to a theory from the 1800s by a guy named Charles Darwin.

If one were to believe the Atheists – and with their already having given us flying horndogs, self-replicating Legos, magic soup, and poetry loving monkeys typing in outer space, who wouldn't? – you'd think that Darwin's theory was the be-all and end-all of science.

Longtime professional atheism enthusiast Daniel Dennett downright gushes over Darwin, calling his theory, "The greatest ever." Not to be outdone by an also-ran, Dawkins goes Dennett even one better. Dawkins declares Darwin's theory to be the greatest theory about anything by anyone who has ever lived, not only on earth but throughout the whole of the heavens, and that it shall be henceforth and forevermore, unto eternity and beyond. Dawkins writes in *The God Delusion*:

> *If a superior creature from the future were to come to earth, the very first question he would ask to judge the level of human civilization would be "have they discovered evolution yet?"*

Just what it is that makes Dawkins believe that he knows what a superior space creature from the future would ask remains an open question, of course, although it does seem to me that there are only three possibilities: either Dawkins believes that he talks to superior space creatures from the future; Dawkins thinks that *he's* a superior space creature from the future or Dawkins is just your typical Militant Atheist trying to pull yet another fast one in the guise of "science."

While it is, of course, standard practice for scientists to cite experts in their field when attempting to prove one or another of their various theories, it does still remain fairly uncommon for one of those experts to be the author's imaginary friend from outer space. Let's call him "Gleebglok."

What is it about these Militant Atheists and superior creatures from outer space, anyway? I wonder if Dawkins thinks that Gleebglok is from Panspermia. If so, he should probably send him a card; after all, they'd be kin! Although I do hope the intergalactic mailman will be alright, what with all of those monkeys flying around in outer space too. If you think that a human being texting while driving on earth is dangerous, just imagine the perils of monkeys typing while careening through the cosmos.

So, what is it about Darwin's theory, then, that sees the Militants engage in such hyperbolic and nonsensical rhetoric on its behalf? The answer is nothing. Sorry, folks, I hate to break it to you, but Dawkins doesn't really pal around with superior space creatures from the future, and Darwin's theory just isn't really anything all that special.

Oh, don't get me wrong, it's a nice theory and all. It might have even helped to have explained a few small things, late in the game and just around the edges, if it were to have turned out to have been right, but the kind of hysteria that sees a so-called "scientist" making a call to authority to a fictional character from outer space on its behalf is nothing other than an obvious case of "Me doth think the lady protests too much."

Clearly there's something about Darwin's theory other than the science that sees the Militants so desperate to have it not only be believed but believed to be the single greatest scientific theory about anything, anywhere, and at any time in the entire history of the universe – past, present, or future – from the lands of Gleebglokia and Panspermia to the shores of Tripoli. So, what is it really?

Before we get into the discussion about what Darwin's theory actually is, we first need to be clear about some of the things that Darwin's theory actually is not – nor did Darwin ever even claim it to be.

For example, Darwin's theory is not actually a theory about the origin of the universe. With or without Darwin, the Atheists' best and only theory about how the universe might have first come into existence without God is still, "Duh, I dunno…shit happens!" and it has been, unchanged, for the past ten thousand years.

Neither is Darwin's theory even an attempt to explain the otherworldly precision of the cosmos. Even if Darwin were to have been spot on in its every jot and tittle, after all of these years, the Atheists' best and only remaining theory on this count is still "ten thousand trillion trillion trillion 'happy accidents'" that then "somehow" "just happened" to have "somehow" "just happened" at least another seven-hundred and ninety-nine more times after that.

It's also not actually a theory about where the DNA's exquisite coding and precision machinery might have come from. Even if Darwin had managed to have nailed it in every conceivable way, the Atheists' best guess on this front is still "monkeys in rooms with typewriters." I think their second-best guess is now "Col. Mustard in the kitchen with a candlestick." I'll have to check on that one.

Contrary to what the Atheists would have you believe, Darwin is also not actually a theory about how life might have first come from the lifeless. In fact, Darwin's theory starts long after Fred's debut and Darwin makes no mention at all of life's beginnings. Yup, with or without Darwin, the Atheists' last remaining theory about how life might have started on earth without God is still "horny aliens from outer space who then had sex with a rock."

Darwin's theory, in fact, is not actually a theory about *any* of the Big Questions nor did Darwin ever claim that it was. It is, in fact, at best, just a small and local theory about a single phenomenon at the very, very, very end of the Atheists in each, and all, and in every way patently absurd origin myth, making the Atheists' obsession with it only that much more curious, still.

Oh, and there's one more fairly significant thing that Darwin's theory actually is not. Darwin's theory is not actually the theory of evolution. The Atheists are desperate for you to believe that it is, but it's not. Darwin didn't actually propose *the* theory *of* evolution; he merely suggested *a* theory *about* evolution.

Darwin no more came up with the concept of evolution than Newton had come up with the concept of gravity. Gravity was the "What is" and then Newton conjectured a "What if?" in an attempt to try and offer a possible means, method, mechanism, or process by which it might work. With Darwin, the "What is" is evolution – the seemingly directed progression of life on earth culminating in the creation of human beings – and then Darwin conjectured a series of mechanisms he theorized might help to explain that phenomenon.

Darwin called these methods and mechanisms that he theorized might help explain how the phenomenon of evolution took place "random mutations," "Natural Selection," and "time." The actual *concept* of evolution was, in fact, first introduced in those very same first few pages of the Bible's book of *Genesis* that has already given us every other significant concept upon which all known science – including Darwin's theory – is then wholly contingent.

The Biblical theory is a far more scientifically sound theory than is Darwin's if only because, while the Biblical theory is comprehensive and explains the evolution – the seemingly directed progression – of everything in the universe, Darwin's is nothing more than a one-time, one-off, ad-hoc theory at the very, very, very end of the Atheists' in each, and all, and in every way patently absurd, wholly unsubstantiated and always extravagantly failed origin myth.

Not only doesn't Darwin's theory even attempt to address any of the Big Questions, then, but, as an ad-hoc theory, it is not applicable to any other phenomenon, big or small, anywhere else in the entire universe either now or ever.

A "one-time," "one-off", and "ad-hoc" theory is the very opposite of a law or a constant and it just doesn't seem to be the sort of thing a superior space creature from the future is likely to have made the trip for. Not even if his frequent flier miles were about to expire. There's something more than just the science!

CHAPTER TWELVE

WRONG AGAIN, NATURALLY

For thousands of years before Darwin came along, farmers and others knew that if they bred two similar plants or animals that had similarly desirable traits, the result was typically the creation of a bigger, stronger, or in some other way better specimen than if the breeding had simply been left to chance. This is the equivalent of Intelligent Design with the farmers using their intelligence to design better – more "evolved" – breeds.

Darwin (amongst many, many others) wondered if the similar progression seen in nature – what we call "evolution" but which is, in fact, just the last part of a fourteen-billion-year-long process – might not be explainable through some sort of materialistic means. This is when Darwin conjured his theory of "'random mutations' acted upon by what he called 'Natural Selection™' over time."

That is Darwin's theory. The "What is" is the seemingly guided better breeding that occurred in nature to produce the various lifeforms and which then culminated in the creation of the human being. Darwin's "What if?" is the combination of the means, methods, mechanisms, and processes of "random mutations," acted upon by "Natural Selection™" over "time."

Perhaps you've already noticed that two of the three mechanisms in Darwin's theory, "random mutations" and "time," is just the same old Infinite Monkey theorem as always, with the word "random" this time simply taking the place of "chance."

This leaves only what Darwin called "Natural Selection™" as the whole of his theory, and the answer can't be found there for the simple reason that that's the question. *Did nature do the kind of selecting that human breeders do?* To this day, the Atheists are still trying to simply make the case that it's not impossible.

Darwin spelled out his theory in his famous book, *On the Origin of Species,* and while it made quite a splash, it didn't really do a very good job of making the case.

For one thing, Darwin's theory has no beginning. In fact, Darwin doesn't even start his theory until after Fred had already "somehow" "just happened" to have "somehow" "just happened" to have been created and had already "somehow" "just happened" to have "somehow" "just happened" to have crawled out of the Magic Soup fully assembled and incredibly complex. Darwin's book says nothing at all about Fred's origin. In fact, Darwin doesn't even once mention Fred's name.

A theory about origins that leaves out the original is not a theory about origins. Whereas the Bible starts its theory about evolution "in the beginning," then, the Atheists start theirs in the middle of the very last part of the very, very, very end.

Having started his story sans beginning, Darwin fails to explain the origin of one of its most essential mechanisms. Darwinian evolution is impossible without the "survival instinct," but Darwin doesn't even attempt to offer a theory as to how this instinct might have first come into being nor how it might work. In fact, the only thing that Darwin's theory makes clear about the survival instinct is the one place we know for sure that it *didn't* come from: Darwinian evolution.

Clearly, if the survival instinct is an essential mechanism for evolution, then it would have had to have "somehow" "just happened" to have been present in the very first lifeform to have "somehow" "just happened" to have "somehow" crawled out of the Magic Soup. Otherwise, Fred wouldn't have evolved into the next lifeform and we'd all still be Freds today. Of course, that wouldn't be all bad; at least we'd all have solar panels!

According to the Atheists, then, Fred would have had to have "somehow" "just happened" to have "somehow" "just happened" to have randomly arisen from the dead, not only self-assembling, self-energizing, self-propelling and self-replicating, but he also would have had to have "somehow" "just happened" to have "somehow" "just happened" to have come into existence already with an instinct for self-preservation.

The existence of the survival instinct poses still yet another major problem for the Atheists. The Atheists' entire gimmick is that the universe is entirely random. That's their whole schtick. If it's not, then it would have had to have been designed. Darwin's theory, however, requires the very purposeful act of seeking to survive. Randomness and purpose, though, are opposites.

So how do the Atheists explain the existence of what they swear doesn't exist, and which, if it does exist wholly debunks their entire origin myth? It depends on where you are. In those places where the Atheists speak Spanish, they say "duh, no sé, la mierda pasa;" in those places where the Atheists speak Finnish, they say "duh, I dunno, en tiedä, paskaa tapahtuu." In the halls of the "evolutionary biology" departments where they speak English, though, the Atheists simply once again just shrug their shoulders and say "Duh, I dunno...shit happens!" The thing that I don't get is, why didn't Dawkins just ask Gleebglok when he had the chance?

The sudden appearance of purpose, is just one of the many, many (many, many) times that something that the Atheists swear doesn't exist anywhere in the universe, and which would totally debunk their entire origin myth if it did, suddenly comes out of nowhere and nothing for no reason and then disappears just as suddenly, once it's been used by the Atheists to save another one of their patently absurd, wholly unsubstantiated, and always extravagantly failed "just-so" stories.

Meanwhile, Fred's having had the incredible luck to have "somehow" "just happened" to have arisen from the dead with an instinct for self-preservation is all well and good, I suppose, but it's not good enough. In order to have survived, Fred would have also have had to have "somehow" "just happened" to have "somehow" "just happened" to have come to life with just the right tools and weapons to have been able to have repeatedly defended himself. Otherwise, he wouldn't have survived long enough to have evolved the next generation. Duh!

In fact, Fred would have had to have been even luckier still because, while tools and weapons are terrific and I highly recommend them, they serve no purpose if you don't know how to use them. Fred, then, would have also have had to have "somehow" "just happened" to have "somehow" "just happened" to have randomly arisen from the dead already skilled in the use of those tools and weapons.

With no beginning, Darwin's theory also lacks for a good ending. How this process of "random mutations" and "Natural Selection™" over time "somehow" "just happened" to have culminated in the human being who "somehow" "just happened" to be able to enjoy the "ingenious illusions" that "somehow" "just happened" to have assembled themselves out of materials that "somehow" "just happened" to have "somehow"" "just happened" to have come out of nowhere and nothing, is just another four-billion-year-long game of Cosmic Craps tacked on at the very, very, very end of the Atheists, in each, and all, and in every other way scientifically and statistically impossible origin myth.

With no beginning and no ending, Darwin's theory also fails to provide very much in the middle. In fact, it barely says anything at all. This is because the descriptions of its key mechanisms – "random" and "natural" – are both just synonyms for "somehow" and "in some way." They're both nothing other than just yet more ways the professional Atheists have for saying, "Duh, I dunno...shit happens!"

Think about it this way. Let's say you and I were at a Penn and Teller show. Near the end of the night, Teller pulls off a rather modest illusion and immediately afterwards I hit you with my elbow and I say, "I know how he did it!"

You're pissed because, well, for one thing, I just hit you with my elbow, but also because I've been annoying you all night, jabbing you after every trick, swearing that I knew how they were all done and every time I'd then said something like "Monkeys with typewriters," "Flying horndogs from outer space," or I just pointed and grunted "Ugg!"

This time, though, I'm particularly insistent. I swear that this time my theory is "the greatest ever!" and, when you balk, I let you in on a little secret: my imaginary friend Gleebglok from the future agrees. You know I'm not going to stop, so you finally nod your ascent.

If I were to then tell you that the rabbit just *randomly* appeared and that it then just *naturally* sawed itself in half, you'd pretty much know that, once again, I didn't actually have even a clue. Well, neither did Darwin. Not even a clue. That's why he used those vague words in the first place.

This is not a swipe at Darwin. Darwin didn't know because Darwin couldn't have known. Darwin's is a theory about genetics conjured at a time when so little was actually known about the workings of the cell, that it was still all thought to be nothing more than just a "gob of goo" which, with regard to Kamala Harris, the case can still be made.

Darwin's is a theory about heredity concocted at a time when the very first hereditary scientist – Gregor Mendel – was still just playing with his very first can of peas and Darwin knew nothing of his efforts.

Darwin used the words "random" and "natural" specifically because, with the science that was known in the 1800s, he had no better way to describe the processes he'd just then totally made up in his head. For some of my younger readers, allow me to put into perspective for you just how far back the 1800s were. They were back before air travel. They were back before electricity. In fact, the 1800s were back even before the 1970s!

What's telling, then, isn't that Darwin's theory is little other than a compendium of synonyms for "Duh, I dunno...shit happens," but rather that the Atheists today must totally ignore everything that's been learned about genetics and heredity since the time of Darwin and Mendel – which is everything that's ever been learned about genetics and heredity – and continue to use the very same vague and meaningless words, "random" and "natural," even though they now know better.

A century-and-a-half after Darwin, the Atheists still have no beginning, the Atheists still have no ending, and the Atheists must still describe the processes in the middle as "random" and "natural," for even just this one-time, one-off, ad-hoc theory at the very, very, very end of their otherwise, and in all other ways, scientifically and statistically impossible origin myth. And this is their *greatest* theory ever, just ask any superior space creature from the future you happen to run into today.

CHAPTER THIRTEEN

NOT RECOMMENDED FOR CHILDREN OVER EIGHT

Given just how little Darwin's theory actually even attempts to address, how small, local, and limited it is in even its hypothetical application, and just how late it appears in the Atheists' in each, and all, and in every way patently absurd origin story, the Atheists' fixation, obsession and, well, downright slobbering over Darwin's theory needs to be explained.

Fortunately, we don't have to speculate about what Darwin's theory does for the Atheists, because Dawkins was kind enough to provide the answer himself. In the chapter of *The God Delusion*, he called "Why are People?", the world's leading spokesmodel for the Atheists' political jihad let the cat out of Schrodinger's bag and, as it turns out, the cat was actually dead the whole time. Dawkins wrote:

Darwin allowed us to give a plausible answer to the curious child.

That's it. That's all it does. Darwin's theory is a just-clever-enough-sounding version of monkeys in rooms with typewriters over time to placate a "curious child." It's just the same old "chance and time" paradigm as always, only in this version "random" gets its big break and takes over the lead role of "chance." Don't worry, though, chance is okay and will be back starring in the Atheists' next production, now in tryouts in New Haven. Rumor has it that this time it's going to be a musical!

Dennett wasn't exactly lying when he called Darwin's theory "The greatest ever." To the Atheists, it *is* the greatest theory ever, but it's not because the theory is so great or that it addresses very much. It's not, it doesn't, and not even Darwin ever suggested that it did. It's because it's the only theory about anything at all, anywhere at all, ever in the history of the universe, that the Atheists can make to sound just scientificky-enough to placate a curious child.

Imagine the horror of being a Militant Atheist "scientist." You know the truth, but because you have a prior commitment to your political jihad, you simply just can't let on. Without Darwin, then, when a curious child asks you, "Why are people, daddy?", all you can say is, "Monkeys in rooms with typewriters, Sally. How many times do I have to tell you! It's ALL monkeys in rooms with typewriters and it is so on every occasion! Now, will you stop asking, damn it!"

Now, at least with Darwin, instead of sending your eight-year-old running off crying "You're so mean, daddy!", you can say "Why that's 'random mutations' acted upon by 'Natural Selection™' over time, sweetheart," and your eight-year-old will say, "You're so smart, daddy! Someday I want to be just like you."

That's it. That's all Darwin's theory does for "science." It allows the Atheists to present the same one and only theory that they have for anything and everything – the same one and only theory that their prior commitment to their political jihad allows them to say that they have for anything and everything – in words that sound just scientificky enough to placate a curious child about this one small question at the very, very, very end of their in each, and all, and in every way scientifically and statistically impossible origin myth.

Of course, even with Darwin, the Atheists still have to worry about the curious child asking about any of the actually big questions. That's the reason Dawkins made the call to his old friend Gleebglok in the first place. After all, if the only thing a superior space creature from the future like Gleebglok needs to know in order to judge the level of our civilization is if we'd discovered "evolution" yet, then that answer should surely be good enough for we inferior earthlings from the ancient present. Now stop asking, damn it!

Sadly, the Gleebglok gambit has worked astonishingly well for the Militants. To many, it really doesn't matter how patently absurd, scientifically impossible, statistically ludicrous, and utterly failed is every part of the Atheists' origin myth – my God, the Atheists can even admit in public journals that their stories are unsubstantiated, failed, and absurd, and exactly why it is that they're peddling them – many people will still judge the level of one's scientific sophistication based entirely on whether or not that person blindly accepts Darwin's theory that the rabbit was just randomly there and that it then just naturally sawed itself in half.

CHAPTER FOURTEEN

MAKING SCIENCE UNSAFE FOR SCIENCE

Having finally found a way to placate the curious child, the Atheists still have a problem, though: what are they to do about the curious *adult*? The Militant Atheists know that they need a way to dissuade those above the age of eight from seeking out and divulging the truth about Darwin's theory.

Thus, in addition to the Big Lie that Darwin had conjured *the* theory *of* evolution and invoking superior space creatures from the future to testify on its behalf, the Militants have engaged in a relentless war of propaganda, lies, deceits, gimmicks, and tricks – and, when all else fails, personal and professional intimidation – to attempt to dissuade, discredit, bully, and destroy the careers of those who dare to expose the truth about Darwinism.

One such deceit, for example, is the Atheists' claim that Darwin's theory is so overwhelmingly supported by so much incontrovertible evidence that it's beyond all possible doubt. "The Science," they say, "is settled!"

Putting aside the fact that there is no more actual science that supports Darwin's theory than there is for any of the Atheists' other theories, and putting aside the fact that, except for in totalitarian regimes, there is no such thing as "The Science," there is also no such thing as "settled science."

This is why long after even the most widely accepted scientific hypotheses have become the "standard model" – things such as Einstein's *theory* about relativity or Newton's *theory* about gravity for example – we still call them "theories." Scientists – real scientists – never say "The Science is settled." Never. Political activists peddling absurd ideological doctrines do. It's their way of saying, "Now stop asking, damn it!"

As the aptly named Martin Brilliant of Bell Laboratories puts it:

> *"Settled science" is a myth, and sometimes a scam. People talk about "settled science" when they want you to believe something. Science is never settled; the best it can achieve is a generally accepted theory.*

"Generally accepted theories" throughout time have included such now discarded notions as that the world is flat, the sun revolves around the earth, and that the Wuhan Virus didn't come from the Wuhan virus laboratory where, at that very moment, they just happened to be making the Wuhan virus.

Akin to and in conjunction with the Militant Atheists' scam that "The Science is settled," is the Militant Atheists' sham that there's some sort of "consensus" on behalf of Darwin's theory. You'll sometimes even hear the Militants say that "every scientist agrees."

Even the marketing gurus at the Trident chewing gum company knew that, for plausibility's sake, they should only claim that *four* out of five dentists recommend sugarless gum to their patients who chew gum, but the Militants need for people to think that there is *no one* who doubts Darwin's theory – not even superior space creatures from the future – because doubt opens the door to questions that the Atheists know that they just don't have even the first clue how to even first start to answer in a way that might even first begin to placate even just a curious first grader.

Meanwhile, even if there were some sort of "consensus" on Darwin's behalf, it still wouldn't save the Atheists. This is because, when it comes to science – real science

– "consensus" is an utterly meaningless concept. In fact, it's not just meaningless; it is *anti*-scientific. Truth isn't a popularity contest and those who claim that it is aren't scientists; they're politicians and propagandists.

The Atheists' use of the Consensus Gambit is a ruse and it is a ruse so long and well known that it actually has a Latin name. It's called "argumentum ad populum." You'll recognize its English translation, "But Mom, everyone else is doing it." If the popularity of a belief proved that belief to be true, then soccer doesn't suck. But soccer *does* suck, and that's a scientific fact.

Here's what Michael Crichton, not only the author of some of the greatest science novels of all time like *Jurassic Park* and *State of Fear* but also, as a Doctor of Medicine, an actual scientist himself has to say about "consensus":

> *Historically, the claim of consensus has been the first refuge of scoundrels; it is a way to avoid debate by claiming that the matter is already settled.*

Scientists – real scientists – don't avoid debate; they seek it out. In fact, debate is the very lifeblood of science. When these Militant Atheist "scoundrels" take refuge behind the fallacious claim of "consensus;" when the same folks who must deny the existence of the laws and constants of science, reject ten thousand years of data, and reverse the protocols of the Scientific Method, they further betray the study of science by shutting down debate.

The Atheists' Consensus gambit is not only antiscientific, though, it is also simply not true. No such consensus exists. Quite to the contrary. Although they might not all admit to it, there is almost no one in the know who doesn't know that Darwin's theory was never fit to survive the rigors of the Scientific Method (or even just plain old common sense.)

This is why Lewontin didn't feel the need to whisper his confession. It's an open trade secret amongst Atheistic "scientists" that Darwinism is a patently absurd construct and a wholly unsubstantiated "just-so" story that has failed extravagantly in its every test. In fact, as an "evolutionary biologist," it is Darwinism that Lewontin was referring to specifically in his confession.

One scientist who doesn't buy into Darwin's vague and ancient theory, for example, is Harvard paleontologist, Stephen Jay Gould. Gould just happens to have been the world's leading paleontologist. Paleontology just happens to be the very field of science that studies the fossil record to see if it comports with one or another theory about how the various lifeforms might have developed over time.

Gould didn't just conclude that Darwin's theory had failed to settle the science; he concluded that the "What is" found in the fossil record over thousands of years of observation, discovery, and experiment – you know, what real scientists call "data" – leaves the "What ifs?" of Darwin's theory wholly debunked.

"Neo-Darwinism is dead," Gould declared. Not "flawed;" not "wounded;" not even "on life support." According to the world's foremost authority on the fossil record, Darwin's theory is *dead*.

Meanwhile, even the professional Atheists themselves tacitly acknowledge that Darwin didn't actually settle the science as they claim. This is why they've been forced to invent a new (or "neo") Darwinism in the first place. It's simply self-evident that one doesn't invent a "neo" theory when the old-o theory had settled the matter. Duh!

Joining the world's leading paleontologist in rejecting both Old-o and Neo-Darwinism is Niles Eldredge. Eldredge just happens to have been the Curator of Invertebrates at the American Museum of Natural History where, amongst other things, he just happened to have helmed the famous Darwin exhibit that travelled the globe to such great acclaim. Eldredge knows his Darwin and Eldredge knows his bones and, because he does, Eldredge knows that the fossil record simply doesn't leave Darwin with even a tibia to stand on:

> *The pattern we were told to find for the past 120 years does not exist.*

Actually, it's now been a hundred and *fifty* years and nothing has changed except for the invention of even more advanced and sophisticated scientific equipment and three more decades of further confirmation that the pattern of slow, gradual change that Darwin's theory predicts and that the scientists were *told* to look for, just does not exist in the fossil record.

Eldredge then went on to describe what the fossil record actually shows:

> *Most evolutionary change occurs in relatively rapid bursts – 5 or 50,000 years – rather than millions of years, where they're typically stable.*

What Gould and Eldredge's works have proved – and which has since been repeatedly confirmed by numerous other observations, discoveries, and experiments (you know, what real scientists call "data" and which will be discussed in detail below) – is that life on earth didn't progress in the slow and steady procession of minor changes Darwin had conjectured way back in the 1800s.

What the fossil record *actually* shows is that there were periods of prodigious and varied creation – one such era being known by both Atheist and believer alike as nothing less than the "Cambrian *explosion*" of lifeforms – and then there were long periods where nothing of significance arose at all. Gould and Eldredge called the pattern actually found in the fossil record, "punctuated equilibrium."

Notable about punctuated equilibrium is that it's not a theory; it's merely a description of the facts. The problem for the Militant Atheists like Lewontin, Dawkins, and Gleebglok, is that the facts fully debunk Darwin's already deeply problematic, terribly vague, and utterly contradictory conjectures.

Since Darwin is the only theory that the Atheists have about anything at all, anywhere at all, at any time at all that might even placate just a curious child, the Militants understood that they must never allow the truth about the fossil record to be known.

The problem for the Militants, though, is that Gould and Eldredge cannot be as easily mocked, bullied, intimidated, and done away with as so many other less well-known scientists have been and continue to be whenever they've exposed the patent absurdities found in Darwin's theory. The works of Gould and Eldredge – alone and together – have made them legends in their fields. Fields, by the way, which Dawkins and Lewontin, as "evolutionary biologists," are simply not a part of.

Dawkins' utter lack of credentials in the field of paleontology didn't stop him from attacking the work of the experts, though, setting off a vicious and legendary battle between Dawkins and Gould, with an enraged Dawkins in the role of Will Smith.

Essentially, Gould was just standing there doing his job when a crazed Dawkins ran up on stage, slapped him in the face, and then returned to the audience shouting vulgarities and self-righteous invectives at him that continue to this day, long after Gould's having passed.

Such rage, of course, is an odd response to a colleague's scientific findings and such emotionalism in the inherently dispassionate world of objective science is still fairly rare. Rage, on the other hand, is the go-to response amongst those attempting to peddle an indefensible political doctrine who know that they can't use their words and their indoor voice to attempt to persuade others because they just don't have the facts to back up their claims. Rage is a way of shutting down debate through bullying and intimidation. See "Antifa" and "BLM" for details.

In *Evolution 2.0* Perry Marshall explains the reason for Dawkins' multi-decade temper tantrum:

> *To suggest that evolution did not occur gradually posed all kinds of new problems for evolutionary theory. Gradualists [Darwinists] considered them [Gould and Eldredge] traitors of sorts.*

Of course, one can only be a "traitor" if they'd been taking sides in the first place. Scientists – real scientists – however, don't take sides; they simply seek out the truth wherever it may lead. Recall from the quotation that started this book, Lewontin freely admits that the Militants "Take the side" of Atheism as simply a matter of course, despite its patent absurdities and unsubstantiated just-so stories that have failed extravagantly whenever they've been tested.

What made Gould and Eldredge "traitors" wasn't that they had somehow betrayed science; it was that, once again, science had betrayed Atheism. Gould was supposed to be a "good soldier" like Lewontin and the army of "We" Lewontin referred to in his article and just shut up and keep the truth to himself for the sake of the Atheists' ideological jihad.

During their famous – and, with Gould remaining a gentleman and a professional throughout, famously one-sided – feud, Dawkins let slip the real reason for his spitting anger. In his book *Unweaving the Rainbow*, the professional Atheist wrote:

> *The extreme Gouldian view...is radically different from and utterly incompatible with the standard neo-Darwinian model. [It] has implications which, once they are spelled out, anybody can see are absurd.*

When I read Dawkins' words, I couldn't help but hear in the author's piteous yowl the voice of Ratso Rizzo, the pathetic street punk from the classic movie, *Midnight Cowboy*, "I'm walking here!" only with Dawkins it was "There's implications here!"

In the movie, Rizzo was reacting to almost being hit by a car; Dawkins, on the other hand, was reacting to having been run down by a truck. Since Darwin is the entirety of Atheistic "science" – the one and only thing that they have that can even possibly placate a small child about even just this one small ad-hoc question – the widespread knowledge of what the fossil record actually shows would be nothing less than catastrophic to the Atheists' political jihad.

Of course, scientists – real scientists – don't oppose the truth because of its implications. Scientists – real scientists – report the truth and let the policy makers then deal with the consequences of reality. To those with a prior commitment to Militant Atheism, however, the implications of Gould and Eldredge's findings and all of the others that have since confirmed them, are just too devastating to their political ends to allow the truth to stand.

The implication that sent Dawkins into such an unprofessional tizzy wasn't just that the one and only theory the Atheists have for anything, anywhere, ever had been disproved, but even more horrifying still, the pattern of prodigious and varied invention followed by long periods of equilibrium that the fossil record actually shows sounds just like those "days" of creation and "nights" of rest first described in the Hebrew Bible.

The professional Atheists desperately cling to Darwin because they all know that the very same book that had gotten everything else right about science from the very beginning and up to this point – which had, in fact, given the world the very concept of science itself – had not only first introduced the concept of evolution, but had then rightly predicted the pattern that science would ultimately confirm from the fossil record some three thousand years later.

Gould's not backing down, then, was seen as a devastating betrayal of the Atheists' political jihad, and if you think that Dawkins was enraged, rumor has it that Glee-bglok was livid. Science had once again pulled itself up over yet another rock, and there they were, those very same theologians from three thousand years earlier, just sitting there waiting as always.

While Gould and Eldredge may be the most prominent scientists to publicly reject Darwin's theory, they are far from the only ones. There are, in fact, well over *two thousand* of the world's leading scientists from the world's most renowned universities and other insti-tutions, across every relevant scientific field who so totally doubt Darwin's small, local, ancient, vague, con-tradictory, and now totally debunked conjectures, that they've signed a statement entitled *A Scientific Dissent from Darwinism*. It says:

> *We are skeptical of claims for the ability of random muta-tion and natural selection to account for the complexity of life. Careful examination of the evidence of Darwinian theory should be encouraged.*

What's particularly odd about this declaration is not that there are thousands of scientists who have thus far signed it; it's that scientists felt the need to write it in the first place. Skepticism should be the very first rule of science, and it should not just be encouraged but it must be expected. Careful examination should simply be a given as the very definition of science itself.

That the simple request for skepticism and careful examination of a theory should require a petition is disturbing enough; what makes it chilling, however, is the caveat its authors felt the need to include at the end:

> *In our experience, expressing dissent from Darwinism can generate controversy and be unsafe, especially for those who haven't earned tenure. If you have not received tenure, you may want to consider carefully whether you should sign.*

In addition to denying the existence of the laws and constants of science, ignoring ten thousand years of data, reversing the Scientific Method, undoing the Enlightenment and silencing debate, the Militant Atheists have made it *unsafe* to employ even the very first rules of science – skepticism and careful examination – when questioning Darwin's theory.

Conversely, it is so safe to outright lie in support of Darwin's theory, that one can state that they are doing just that, as simply a matter of course, in the pages of the *New York Review of Books* without even the slightest fear of personal or professional recrimination.

If tenure can be used as a benchmark of academic achievement, then *thousands* of the world's most accomplished scientists join Gould and Eldredge – the leaders in their two respective fields – in publicly disbelieving Darwin's ancient theory enough to risk the wrath of the Militants by signing onto the dissent.

Given that only a very tiny percentage of scientists ever receive tenure, the fact that well over two thousand of them have signed onto the petition makes it clear that there are likely tens of thousands of others who, having not yet received the protections that tenure can provide them from the Militants, have heeded the warning of their colleagues and have kept the truth to themselves.

When one then adds to that the number of Militant Atheists like Lewontin and all of the others he refers to in his confession as "we" who admit to knowing the truth, but who have a "prior commitment" to their political jihad, we're now talking about many, many thousands more.

If Darwin's theory were any other theory, it would have been discarded a hundred years ago. The problem is that Darwin's theory is the only theory the professional Atheists have about anything, anywhere, ever, and thus they simply cannot let go.

And the funniest part of it all? Remember how Darwin starts long after Fred "somehow" "just happened" to "somehow" "just happened" to have come alive long before Darwin's tale starts? Well, even for the Atheists to tell this one-time, one-off, ad-hoc story that doesn't even address any of the Big Questions and, as an ad-hoc theory, cannot be applied to any of the other small ones, either, the Atheists needed a preexisting life to whom they could then ascribe the intelligence to know both to defend and *how* to defend himself, and then be selective in his choice of prey. Even when the Atheists are trying to sell you Darwin, they are yet again reconfirming the fundamental tenets of Intelligent Design and the revelations of the Bible.

Meanwhile, even in attempting just to placate the curious child, Dawkins had been forced to lie. Darwin's theory does nothing whatsoever to answer the question "Why are people?" "Why" isn't even a question Atheists allow to be asked, for the simple reason that reason and randomness are opposites.

At best, if Darwin's theory had turned out to have been right, it might have helped to have answered the question "*how* are people?", but even then, the best the Atheists would have to offer would still be nothing other than "randomly" and "naturally," or, to put it another way, "Duh, I dunno...shit happens. Now stop asking, damn it!"

CHAPTER FIFTEEN

AND THE BEST DIRECTOR AWARD GOES TO...

The greatest irony with regard to Darwin's theory is that it's not the believer in either the science of Intelligent Design in general or even the specific God of the Bible but the atheist who cannot honestly believe in evolution, Darwinian or other.

Even if Darwin's theory had turned out to have been right, it wouldn't have served to have diminished God's majesty even in the slightest. As the deeply religious Charles Kingsley wrote upon the publication of *On the Origin of Species*:

> *[It is] just as noble a conception of Deity, to believe that He created primal forms capable of self-development... as to believe that He required a fresh act of intervention to supply the lacunas which He Himself had made.*

After looking up the word "lacunas," I had to agree.

Perhaps no better evidence for the fact that there is no intellectual distance between Darwin's theory, were it to have been right, and belief in God can be found than in the fact that Alfred Russel Wallace, Darwin's collaborator (and sometimes competitor) had no doubt whatsoever, not only about the existence of a creator, but that that creator was a God just like the one in the Bible. Here's what Charles H. Smith, Ph.D., the world's foremost authority on Wallace wrote:

> [O]f course, he undoubtedly accepted that behind all "universal forces and laws" there lay "the will or power" of a "Great Mind" or "Supreme Intelligence."

The words in the quotation marks are Wallace's.

Well, maybe there's *one* thing that better serves as evidence that belief in Darwin's theory had it been right, and belief in God are not in the least bit incompatible: Darwin himself believed in God, and he did so long after he'd come up with his theory. In fact, in his autobiography, written near the end of his life, Darwin said:

> [My belief in God] follows from the extreme difficulty or rather impossibility of conceiving this immense and wondrous universe, including man with his capacity of looking

backwards and far into futurity, as a result of blind chance or [mere] necessity.

In fairness, Darwin did sometimes have his doubts about God, and he often went back and forth over the course of his lifetime between identifying himself as an "agnostic" and a "deist," but one thing for sure, he never was an atheist, much less a militant one.

In fact, unlike the professional Atheists who today cynically peddle Darwin's theory as the be-all and end-all of science, Darwin did not believe that his theory had "settled the science" about even just this one small question, much less about any of the Big Ones. In fact, being a real scientist, Darwin not only encouraged debate about the validity of his theory, he often led it.

Darwin was well-aware of the fact that many of the relevant fields of scientific inquiry like paleontology and heredity were only then still in their infancy, and that he knew nothing at all about the actual workings of the cell, leaving his theory, as he well understood, little more than clever but wholly unsubstantiated conjecture.

Thus Darwin, whose "prior commitment" was to science, voiced numerous and significant doubts about his own theory, suggesting that if certain things were to be revealed in the future by these new fields of inquiry and the use of more advanced and sophisticated equipment and techniques, his conjectures will have been proved to have been wrong. These things have, in fact, now been repeatedly found. In fact, they've typically proved to be the norm. Meyer writes extensively about Darwin's doubt in a book the author brilliantly entitled *Darwin's Doubt*.

Meanwhile, Wallace didn't have any doubts at all about his and Darwin's theory being the be-all and end-all of science; he downright repudiated the very notion:

> *[Many human] physical characteristics are not explicable on the theory of variation and survival of the fittest.*

"Variation" is what is said to have been created by those "random mutations;" the "survival of the fittest" is the mechanism that the theory hypothesizes is what powers "Natural Selection™."

The irony, then, is not just in the fact that both of the inventors of Darwin's theory believed in God and had significant doubts about their own conjectures (as did every other one of Darwin's numerous collaborators), nor is it just that those who believe in the God of the Bible need not have any intellectual problem with the concept of Darwinian evolution had it proved to have been right; it is in the fact that, it is those who swear that they have no doubts at all – the Atheists – who cannot honestly believe in evolution of any kind. This is because evolution – by its very definition – implies a direction.

There is simply no known law or laws of any of the known sciences nor a single observation, discovery, or experiment – you know, what real scientists call "data" – from over the course of the past ten thousand years, that allows for direction without a directing force. Even when there is a directing force, if it's not an intelligent one, then all you'll end up with is something like Steven Spielberg's *West Side Story*. The Atheists cannot believe in evolution, Darwinian or other, for the simple reason that randomness and direction are opposites. Duh!

Worse still for the Atheists is the fact that this direction is qualitative. The word "evolution" implies a steady line of *improvement*. Its opposite is *devolution*. Randomness doesn't have an opposite direction because it's random. Duh again.

The Atheists are so well-aware of just how existential a threat this obvious contradiction is to Darwinism that Harvard "evolutionary biologist," Robert Trivers, didn't wait even a single paragraph in his introduction to Dawkins' giant book of patently absurd "What ifs?", *The Selfish Gene*, before addressing it. He wrote:

> *There exists no objective basis on which to evaluate one species above another.*

While I will agree with Trivers that it is often difficult to tell the difference between a parasite and a politician,

I do believe that if a possum were to walk into the DMV to get a driver's license, even an "evolutionary biologist" would have no problem determining that it simply just wasn't up to the task. Just trying to get the possum to recite the lines on the eye chart would likely serve as a tipoff to most.

So, then, can Trivers really not tell the qualitative difference between, say, a species that pairs fine wines as it sups on beef bourguignon and one that drinks from the toilet and eats its own feces? If so, while I'd be happy to debate him at any time, I'm not soon going to be accepting an invitation to dinner at the Trivers' home.

Trivers' claim is not merely patently absurd, though, it is also the very fount of all that is evil. If one truly believes that there is no objective qualitative difference between the species, then murdering a child would be no different than swatting a fly and genocide would be no worse than calling the exterminator. As we shall see, it is not a coincidence that the very same Atheists who must deny the existence of God and science, must then replace them with the most unscientific and evil of all concepts. It, as we shall see, it is the cause of the evils that are wracking America and the West, today.

So, on what basis, then, does Trivers make his claim that has such dire moral implications if it were to be accepted as true? I'll let Trivers tell you himself:

> *To an evolutionist [Darwinist], man's superiority simply cannot be so.*

That's it. Trivers simply decrees it. Trivers simply starts with the Militant Atheists' political doctrine, and then, when the facts get in the way, he just eliminates the self-evident from the left side of the Atheists' "scientific" ledger. The same folks whose only defense of the patently absurd is to declare that *anything*'s possible, must at the same time decree that the self-evident, "simply cannot be so."

The evolution of the various species is obviously qualitative. This is why so few people would want to change places with a squid, with the possible exception of Brian Stetler who, by all appearances, already has.

While the Atheist is forced to, at once, embrace patent absurdities and deny self-evident realities, the believer has no such problem. The Bible makes very clear what we all see with our eyes, understand with our reason, and embrace with our morality: obviously there is a qualitative hierarchy amongst the animals and clearly man is at the very, very top.

This is why so few people have pet ants, but so many people do have pet dogs and it's why those dogs are our pets and, with the exception of some folks on the Upper West Side of Manhattan, it's not the other way around. If you really can't tell the qualitative difference between a human being and a warthog, it might just help to explain why your Tinder dates keep turning out so badly for you.

While Trivers was obviously trying to help make the case for Darwin's theory, in reality, he succeeded only in entirely debunking it in just one sentence. If, in order for Darwin to be so, man cannot be objectively qualitatively above the other species and man is, in fact, objectively qualitatively above the other species, then, according to Trivers himself, Darwinism simply cannot be so. I'll be happy to change my mind the very next time I see a possum with even just a learner's permit.

Making matters even worse still for the Atheists, is that not only does evolution move in a direction and not only is that direction qualitative, but, according to all known science, it moves in the *wrong* direction.

The laws and constants of science makes clear that over time things tend to go from the complex to the simple – from the organized to the chaotic – and not the other way around. This just happens to be the second law of thermodynamics and the first law of In-and-Out burger.

Anyone who has ever eaten at an In-and-Out burger knows that over time, far from a Double-Double evolving into a more complex and better organized sandwich, in almost no time at all it becomes a bigger mess than the sleeve of a millennial who's just been told "no." The only way for a Double-Double to become bigger or better organized is for an intelligent lifeform – or at least the kid working behind the counter – to come along and act upon it.

While Alexandria Ocasio-Cortez might serve as the exception that proves the rule, living things are significantly more complex than a hamburger, but the science remains the same. Things in this universe don't, on their own, tend to evolve over time into more complex or better organized things. In fact, without an intelligent, outside force acting upon them, things tend to *devolve* over time, like an abandoned car on a redneck's front lawn or the second day of a socialist's ten-year plan.

CHAPTER SIXTEEN

HOW DARWIN WORKS (SPOILER ALERT: IT DOESN'T)

Whenever you come across someone who pats themselves on the back for their atheism, saying that (unlike you) they "believe in science," there are two things that you can instantly be sure of 1) The only "science" that they know is Darwin's theory and 2) They don't know anything at all about Darwin's theory.

It's not their fault. How many of us did? How many of us didn't just simply take the science book's word for it when we were seven or eight years old, and have never given it even another moment's thought since? I did. Until I gave it another moment's thought. There's very good reason that the Militants are so desperate to not allow it to be debated. It's because Lewontin was telling the truth: the theory is patently absurd, wholly unsubstantiated, and extravagantly failed in its every test.

The Atheists' theory is that random changes occur in an organism when, at no particular interval and for no particular reason, random letters "spontaneously" insert themselves (or delete themselves) from the DNA code that controls all aspects of the body's development and operation. The Atheists don't have even a clue as to how or why these mutations take place. In fact, "spontaneous" is just another word the Atheists use when they mean to say "Duh, I dunno...shit happens!"

This errant code, they say, then "somehow" "just happens" to "somehow" "just happens" to cause a tiny change in the body of that one individual being that might, in "some or another way," "somehow" "just happen" to provide that one lone member of that one lone species with "some sort" of random advantage in its daily struggle to survive.

Here, again, I don't say "somehow," "some sort" and "in some or another way" just because *I* don't know; I say it because, here again (and as always), *they* don't know. The professional Atheists have no more of a clue as to how any mutation might aid in the survival of a member of a species or a species as a whole than they do about anything else.

When the Atheists describe the Darwinian process as "the survival of the fittest," even they admit that they haven't even a clue as to how that being survived. Instead, by their own admissions, they've simply decreed that that which survived is, ipso facto, the fittest. This designation is assigned *post facto* without any other evidence of the being's "fitness" than the fact that it survived. Both ipso facto *and* post facto; man, they're good!

The very definition of Darwin's theory as it is best understood by most, then, is nothing more than a mere and meaningless tautology – "that which survived is the fittest to have survived." Meanwhile, no means, method, mechanism, or process for how that survival might have taken place is even in the offing. It's still all just "random" and "natural" or, to put it another way, "Duh, I dunno...shit happens!"

In fact, Darwin didn't even actually insert the phrase "the survival of the fittest" into *On the Origin of Species* until the fifth edition, preferring to describe the process in his first four tries as being the survival of those "best adapted" to their environment.

The problem, Darwin realized, is that while "the survival of the fittest" is a meaningless tautology, the survival of those "best adapted" is a contradiction of Darwin's most basic premise. This is because randomness and adaptation are opposites. By definition, things don't randomly adapt.

Having swung and missed in their first two attempts to simply provide even the most basic description of Darwin's theory, the one that is most en vogue amongst the professional Atheists today is that, "Those that have the most offspring that survive are the ones that have the most offspring that survive." It's *still* just a meaningless tautology and it *still* fails to even suggest a means, method, mechanism, or process by which survival takes place. Besides, as anyone who has ever been to a Target store on a Saturday knows, just because something has a lot of offspring that survived, it doesn't mean that that offspring is in any way evolved.

Despite the fact that these mutations are said to be random, the theory is that every once in a while, one of them "somehow" "just happens" to be just that one tiny indispensable little thingy that is "just so" to "somehow" "just happen" to make that one individual member of that one species "in some way" more "fit" to survive than are its brethren who are in every other significant way exactly like him. It's a rather odd claim on any number of fronts.

For one thing, nature isn't monolithic. Things die in tens of thousands of different ways. Twice that if you live in Chicago. Even if, as luck would have had it, that latest random mutation had "somehow" "just happened" to have "somehow" "just happened" to have made that one individual member of that one lone species "in some way" just a tiny bit more "fit" to survive one peril, it would have done nothing at all to have improved its odds against all of those other menaces found in nature. In fact, it would only have made it even *more* susceptible to those other and far more numerous threats.

A tad more fat that randomly popped out around the middle of a penguin in the arctic, for example, might theoretically have been just sufficient enough to have, perhaps, seen that one lone penguin survive a slightly colder winter, but it also would have made it the least fit to have survived a typically warm summer.

At the same time, that same random roll of fat that would have made that one penguin the warmest of its kind, also would have made it the *slowest* of its kind and thus the *most* likely to have been tracked down by its numerous predators. This doesn't even begin to take into account the 9,999 other perils that the additional roll of fat does nothing to address, including dying of embarrassment whenever swimsuit season came around.

Even this, of course, is only if that roll of fat "somehow" "just happened" to have "somehow" "just happened" to have randomly popped out in the penguin's middle and not in any of the tens of thousands of other places that it might just as likely have randomly popped out of, such as the penguin's liver, spleen, kidneys, heart, lungs, eyes, throat, spine, ankle, hip, knee, brain, toe, shin, calf, scalp, or whatever that little thingy is called on the back of a penguin's elbow.

The notion that these random mutations are each "just that one tiny indispensable little thingy" that that one specific individual needs to survive is further belied by the fact that, just the day before that last lucky random mutation occurred, all of the others of that species were themselves the fittest to – and did – survive just fine. In fact, many from those "less fit" lines continue to survive just fine to this day.

Making Darwin's story even more implausible still, is the fact that, according to his theory, these random mutations are said to produce only the most miniscule of changes. Sometimes people are fooled into believing the notion that the fittest survive because they look at the very end of the evolutionary process, where it's easy to see how a giraffe's elongated neck or an elephant's powerful trunk might well be sufficiently advantageous to explain that species' survival.

Darwin's theory, however, doesn't claim that large and significant changes occur. The Bible does. The fossil record does. Gould and Eldredge's combined seventy-five years of impeccable research as well as the works of thousands of tenured professors at the world's most renowned institutions does, but Darwin's theory doesn't.

Instead, Darwin conjectured that these mutations created only the tiniest of changes, which are said to have then "somehow" "just happened" to have "somehow" "just happened" to have randomly accrued, little by little, over the course of the next four billion years until they "somehow" "just happened" to have "somehow" "just happened" to have become the very species that a believer in the God of the Bible would expect.

Obviously, the odds of these trillions and trillions (and trillions and trillions) of random mutations having "somehow" "just happened" to have "somehow" "just happened" to have, then, created the human being are beyond astronomical, to which must not only be added, but be multiplied by the statistical impossibilities of every other part of the Atheists' origin myth to this point. And the odds aren't even anywhere near as good as that for the Atheists.

This is because not only would every one of these trillions and trillions (and trillions and trillions) of random mutations have had to have "somehow" "just happened" to have "somehow" "just happened" to all of just the right ones; they also would have all had to have "somehow" "just happened" to have "somehow" "just happened" all in just the right order.

While perhaps it's not impossible (you know, if it wasn't impossible) that a new sprig of nose hair might have "somehow" "just happened" to have "somehow" "just happened" to have randomly popped out on some creature along the way and, in having done so, made that one creature just the tiniest bit more "fit" to have survived that winter's cold and flu season; that would only be true, though, if that species had already "somehow" "just happened" to have "somehow" "just happened" to have randomly popped out a nose.

If that very same sprig of hair had "somehow" "just happened" to have randomly popped out *before* the nose, though, not only would it have served no evolutionary purpose, it would have just looked like a Hitler moustache, which is never a good thing, unless you happen to be running for president of a national teachers' union.

The first part of Darwin's theory – random mutations over time – is nothing other than the same old Infinite Monkey theorem, as always with the trillions and trillions (and trillions and trillions) of random mutations having all "somehow" not just "somehow" "just happened" but all of them then having "somehow" "just happened" to have "somehow" "just happened" all in just the right order.

Obviously the odds of all that having "somehow" "just happened" to have "somehow" "just happened" is effectively zero and that zero is then not just added to but multiplied by every one of the other steps in the Atheists' origin myth that are each, and all effectively zero. And that, of course, is only if any part of it was even possible. Not even one part of it is possible. Yeah, it's those pesky laws and constants of science again.

When a complex and well-organized system like the DNA's computer code is randomly mutated, it doesn't create a more complex or better organized system. In fact, all known science across every known field of science, as well as literally every observation, discovery, and experiment – you know, what real scientists call "data" – going all the way back to the very first day of the world's very first caveman, makes clear that it does exactly the opposite. Things that are well organized are only made less organized when random things are, then, introduced.

If you don't believe me; try it yourself. Since this is the first law of In-and-Out Burger, go to an In-and-Out restaurant and get yourself a Double-Double. Next, put it down on a flat, dry surface. Maybe something like a table that has randomly and spontaneously just naturally appeared out of nothing and nowhere and, by happy accident, just happens to be somewhere nearby. Hey, you can't prove that it *didn't* happen!

Now randomly mutate the sandwich by kicking the table's leg. The Atheists entire argument when it comes to Darwin's theory is that, if you kept kicking the table's leg for "enough" time, it's not impossible that not only would the sandwich become better organized, but that you might even eventually just randomly add pickles and relish to it as well.

No matter what the Atheists say, a runaway shopping cart in a supermarket parking lot that randomly mutates your old Buick won't turn it into brand-new Porsche. Not even after a million, billion, trillion, gazillion years. What it will do at some point, though, is turn your old Buick into an inoperable clunker.

Monkeys inserting random letters into a well-written book wouldn't turn that book into the collective works of Shakespeare. What it would do, and do rather quickly, though, is turn that well-written book into utter gibberish. You know, if there were monkeys in outer space and they knew how to type.

Well, inserting (or deleting) random letters in a computer code like that of the DNA wouldn't create a bigger or better running program; what it would do – and do quickly – is crash the computer. The reason for this is simple, obvious: it's because the operating system in the cell that had, until then, been working just fine, wouldn't be able to read the increasingly random code. Dxvumeh!

CHAPTER SEVENTEEN

WHOM'S ON FIRST

Since Darwin's theory is only a two-mechanism process and the first mechanism fails extravagantly, a means, method, mechanism, or process for Darwinian evolution had better be found in "Natural Selection™." It's not. "Natural Selection™" fails extravagantly, too. You know, if it wasn't also impossible.

The problem with "Natural Selection™" only starts with the obvious fact that there's simply no such thing. At least not according to the Atheists. Haven't the Atheists been telling us this whole time that everything in the universe is random? Isn't that their entire schtick? Suddenly, this one time, out of nowhere and for no reason luck "just happened" to have "somehow" "just happened" to have created discernment? It's not nature that's selective, it's the Atheists' arguments that are. Discernment and randomness are opposites. Duh!

Where do the Atheists even say that nature's ability to be discerning might have come from, anyway? There's nothing in Darwin's theory that even addresses it, and Darwin's theory is all the Atheists have. In fact, the *only* thing that Darwin's theory even suggests about the origin of "nature's" ability to discern is that, like the survival instinct, it didn't come about through Darwinian evolution.

Clearly, if selectivity is essential to the evolutionary process, it would have had to have "somehow" "just happened" to have "somehow" "just happened" to have been present in the very first living thing. Otherwise, Fred wouldn't have evolved, and we'd all still be Freds today. Of course, that wouldn't be all bad; at least we'd finally all have solar panels.

According to the Atheists, then, not only did Fred "somehow" "just happen" to randomly arise from the dead and then "somehow" "just happen" to crawl out of the Magic Soup self-assembling, self-energizing, self-propelling, and self-replicating with the instinct, weaponry, and skills for self-defense, he would also have had to have "somehow" "just happened" to have "somehow" come to life with the self-discipline to be selective. What a guy! I simply can't understand why he never found a wife. Oh, right, there were no other fish in the sea yet. In fact, according to the Atheists, there wasn't even a sea. Just a big old bowl of Magic Soup.

Meanwhile, how would nature even know how to be selective? After all, many living things don't even have a brain, such as plants, shrubs, and half of all Yale law school graduates; or else they have teeny-weenie and almost entirely useless brains like ticks, mites, and the other half of all Yale law school graduates.

Is there even any objective reason to believe that nature *is* selective? It sure doesn't look that way to me. Have you ever seen those bears that stand over the river as the salmon just jump into their mouths? Have you ever seen an aardvark stick its tongue down an anthill? Have you ever seen Jack Black eat lunch? The reality is that nature is just not all that selective. In fact, nothing in the known universe is more selective than Martha Stewart, and even she's been seen hanging around with Snoop Dogg from time to time.

Meanwhile, "nature" is more than just living things. I don't think even the Atheists claim that the inanimate forces of nature like monsoons and tsunamis, tornadoes and cyclones are discerning. It wouldn't surprise me if they did – these folks will say anything – I'm just saying that I'm not aware of it.

The reality is that no new sprig of nose hair, slightly longer toenail, or miniscule new roll of fat makes even the slightest bit of difference against these titanic forces of nature. In fact, not even the Titanic could withstand the titanic forces of nature and it was titanic. Against these immense powers of nature even the "fittest" of the species gets blown away like a leaf in a hurricane or a girl in a girl's swim meet.

Meanwhile, every time that nature gets it wrong and "selects" that one otherwise impossibly lucky individual with that latest lucky evolutionarily advanced mutation, it puts an end to that evolutionary line, sets the already impossible timetable back yet again, spins evolution off in yet another random direction, and renders the odds of the whole process culminating in the audience at Penn and Teller's midnight show, only that much more impossible still.

As patently absurd as is the notion that nature is selective, the truth is that even if nature were more discriminating than even John Legend in a Neiman Marcus, it still wouldn't save Darwinism. This is because, according to Darwin's theory, the process of "Natural Selection™" possesses no evolutionary powers.

In Darwin's theory *all* evolutionary change is caused by the random mutations. They're the shopping carts that the Atheists swear turn Buicks into Porsches. In Darwin's theory, all that "Natural Selection™" is said to do is tow the old clunkers away for demolition.

Since "random mutations over time" is just another version of the Infinite Monkey theorem and the process of "Natural Selection™" has no evolutionary powers, far from Darwin's theory being the Atheists' *greatest* theory ever, it's nothing other than the same old theory as always – chance and time.

In fact, since the *only* thing that makes Darwin's theory in any way different from all of the Atheists other theories about anything, anywhere, ever, is the addition of "Natural Selection™," and since, in the real world, nature often hauls off the Porsche by mistake, Darwin's theory is actually the *worst* theory the Atheists have ever yet tried to peddle.

Think about it this way, the first part of Darwin's theory is still just the same old monkeys as always, typing their little hearts away in outer space; the only difference is that this time they've thrown in some gorillas who go around ripping papers out of the machines.

CHAPTER EIGHTEEN

SCIENCE – REAL SCEINCE

Meanwhile, back in the real world, the evidence against the Atheists' only theory about anything, anywhere, ever, just keeps rolling in:

> *Darwin's theory of evolution bases its main tenet on the premise that genes emerge randomly... This fundamental assumption has now been disproved.*

Who disproved it? How about a team consisting of scientists from the Max Planck Institute of Biology, the Carnegie Institute for Science, the University of California, Davis and Stanford University. I get that they're not superior space creatures from the future, but they're the very best scientists that we have on earth at this time.

If you're not impressed by those credentials, then how about America's foremost scientific institution, the National Academy of Sciences?

In research that will help address a long-running debate and apparent contradiction between short- and long-term evolutionary change, scientists have discovered that although evolution is a constant and sometimes rapid process, the changes that hit and stick tend to take a long time.

The language in this article is a tad confusing since there's no such thing as "short-term" (Darwinian) evolution. If evolution happened rapidly, it's not Darwinian. What the writer means is that small – often cosmetic – changes occur from generation to generation. Well, duh. Who looks exactly like their grandfather except maybe Liz Cheney?

Mere change is not Darwinian evolution. Darwinian evolution implies a steady and consistent pattern of directional progress, and this massive study conducted by the nation's top scientific institution only, yet again, reconfirms the works of Gould and Eldredge and the tens of thousands of others that makes clear that that pattern simply does not exist.

At the same time, if there's evolutionary change but it doesn't "stick," it's not Darwinian either. Darwin's theory requires a long, steady, and uninterrupted progression, not a series of fits and starts. In fact, "a series of fits and starts" sounds a whole lot like the "creation and rest" found in the Bible, and not just to me but to Josef Uyeda, the lead author of the National Academy of Sciences' report. Uyeda concluded:

> *This research supports the overall pattern of stasis [equilibrium] and punctuational change.*

Meanwhile, of the three elements in the Atheists' Infinite Monkey theorem, only one of them is real. It's not the monkeys writing Elizabethan poetry and it's not the typewriters floating around in outer space; it's time. Well, according to this definitive study from America's premier scientific institution, Darwin's theory simply does not stand up to its test.

Another recent challenge to Darwin's theory came and went in the news so quickly that perhaps some of you might have missed it. It was a little something they called the "Coronavirus pandemic." Maybe you remember, it was on the Internet for a while and everything. Remember? Facebook even allowed some parts of it to be talked about, like the fact that the Wuhan virus didn't come from the Wuhan virus laboratory but from a bat that "just happened" to be just down the street. Oh, come on, think back. After that, the "fact-checkers" cut off debate because they said that "The Science" was settled. You remember. Then they made it unsafe for anyone who dared to speak the truth about it by threatening their livelihoods and cutting off their access. Oh, sure you remember the Coronavirus panic, don't you?

Well, each of the variants of the Coronavirus that followed so closely one after the other did so in utter opposition to Darwin's theory. The Darwinian process is said to be slow, gradual and random with just the slightest incremental change over an excruciatingly long period of time. You know, sort of like an episode of *Yellowstone*. These mutant strains, however, were created quickly and specifically for a purpose: to adapt to the immunities the human body had created to fight them. Purpose and randomness are opposites. Randomness and adaptation are opposites, too. Duh and even Duhmer!

The fact that not all of these strains became bigger, better, smarter, stronger, faster, more complex or in any way more discerning is just yet another strike against the line of slow and steady progress around which Darwin's entire theory revolves.

It's not just viruses that change rapidly to adapt to their situation, either. So, too, does the human immune system tasked with fighting off these and other maladies. This is from a recent article in *Salon* magazine:

> *A peculiar study into malaria resistance in humans and where and how it occurs in the population, has unexpect-*

edly spurred a re-evaluation of the Neo-Darwinist understanding of evolution.

I guess the Atheists are going to have to make up a neo-Neo-Darwinism.

While *Salon* tends to be just above *Highlights* when it comes to intellectual sophistication, their story this time turns out to be right. The only thing they got wrong is that there was nothing actually "peculiar" about the study. It was, in fact, conducted in exactly the way that all real science – but not Atheistic "science" – is conducted: using the Scientific Method.

What makes the results "peculiar" and "unexpected" to the writer is that, if one hasn't given much thought to Darwin's theory – perhaps doesn't even know that Darwinism is nothing more than just a theory – the findings are not what one would expect. To the rest of us, though, there was nothing peculiar about the study nor unexpected in the results.

Dr. Adi Livnat from the University of Haifa, the lead researcher and co-author of the paper told Salon:

This sort of result cannot be explained by Neo-Darwinism... [It] challenges the very notion of random mutation on a fundamental level.

Darwin's theory not only extravagantly fails in its every test on earth; it fails extravagantly whenever it's been tested in outer space, as well. Take *that*, Gleebglok (and Panspermians beware; we're in outer space now and we haven't forgotten what you did!!!).

Prior to Scott Kelly's ascending to power as a radical Leftist senator from Arizona, he spent a year on the International Space Station as a radical Leftist astronaut. Scientists conducted experiments on the effects that his brief time outside of the earth's gravity had on his body, and here's how *Newsweek* summed up their findings:

> *NASA astronaut Scott Kelly's body altered its own gene expressions in just one year! His body executed a direct evolutionary response to the rigors of the International Space Station.*

One suspects that the writer threw in the word "evolutionary" so as not to incur the wrath of the Militants as a "direct response" is the very opposite of a *random* mutation, while the mere one-year time frame in which Kelly's genes mutated, is the very opposite of the slow and incremental change that Darwin's theory predicts and without which Darwin's theory fails entirely (thus, the writer's use of the exclamation point!).

These adaptations weren't the result of a single, lucky, random mutation, either. In fact, a full *seven percent* of

Kelly's genes altered their function in direct response to his new environmental realities. These same results have been repeatedly confirmed in all fourteen of the other astronauts who have since been similarly studied.

Both the rapid timeframe and the fact that random mutations don't adapt to the environment sees Darwin, in just this one test alone, debunked yet again, twice over and in outer space, no less. Making matters even worse for the Atheists is that, in the entire time that Kelly and the other astronauts were in orbit, not once did any of them report seeing a typing monkey, a horny space alien, or any one of Gleebglok's ancient ancestors, much less a rabbit that just randomly appeared and then just naturally sawed itself in half.

The fact that the professional Atheists must portray Darwin – a vague and ancient theory that doesn't even attempt to address any of the Big Questions and which, as an ad-hoc theory, is not and cannot even be applied to any other question, big or small – as the be-all and end-all of science, should be understood for what it is: the professional Atheists' confession that Darwin's theory is all that the Atheists have to even try to explain even the smallest of things. Anywhere. Ever.

At the same time, the lengths the professional Atheists must go to – the deceits, the lies, the gimmicks, and the tricks (not to mention the personal and professional intimidation) – to not allow for even skepticism about, much less careful consideration of, Darwin's theory should be recognized for what *it* is. It is the professional Atheists' confession that not even they believe it. In fact, just as Lewontin publicly confesses, they know Darwin's theory to be just another one of their wholly unsubstantiated and extravagantly failed "just-so" stories that is, at once, statistically and scientifically impossible in each and every one of its parts.

Oh, and one last thing. The only reason the Atheists even have this one, small, local, vague, and utterly absurd theory at all, is because God (or luck) provided them with a preexisting lifeform in Fred, to whom they could then ascribe the intelligence to know both to and how to defend itself and to be discerning in its choice of prey. Where that lifeform came from, the Atheists don't know and how it came to be intelligent the Atheists don't say. All Darwin proves is that, once again, the Atheists can't even conjure a story without, yet again, reconfirming the basic tenets of the science of Intelligent Design in general and the God of the Bible in particular.

CHAPTER NINETEEN

LET'S GET METAPHYSICAL

We are still clueless how the brain represents the content of our thoughts and feelings
– "Evolutionary Psychologist" and Militant Atheist Steven Pinker.

If the professional Atheists can't even first begin to explain the creation and design of the things in the physical universe, their efforts are only even more doomed (as if that were possible) when we begin to talk about the fifth and final of the Big Question, the existence of the metaphysical.

The word "metaphysical" is derived from the Latin meaning "beyond the physical" and, unsurprisingly, the existence of such traits as self-awareness, creativity, love, and empathy – the very things that do, in fact, make we humans objectively and qualitatively superior to rocks, toads, and fans of the Dave Mathews band – is entirely beyond those whose political agenda requires them to deny that anything beyond the physical exists.

Thus, to this day, as the famed Militant Atheist Steven Pinker admits in the quotation above, the Atheists still don't have even the first clue as to the means, methods, mechanisms or processes that give we humans consciousness and allow us to think and feel.

This, then, yet again, sees the world's very first caveman far ahead of today's Atheistic "scientists." After all, they both have exactly the same degree of knowledge about the origin of thoughts and feelings but only the Atheists have college loans to repay.

In fairness, the Atheists are a tad more advanced than was the world's very first caveman when it comes to knowing where these traits might have first come from in that they, at least, have a single clue. The Atheists know the one place that they definitely *didn't* come from: Darwinian evolution.

The fact that the metaphysical traits suddenly first appear at the very, very, very end of the evolutionary line makes undeniable that they're not a requisite for survival. If they were, then none of the species that came before us would have survived, we wouldn't be here, and I'd have wasted a great deal of my time in having written this book.

Some will claim that the metaphysical traits like love and compassion exist in a few of the lesser species just a little further back down the evolutionary line like cats, dogs, and people who eat Spam. The problem is that even if Mimi, Moo Moo, and Earl were to possess some of the metaphysical traits, all that this would do is double the Atheists' already astounding woes.

First the Atheists would need to explain the sudden (non-evolutionary) appearance of these traits in the higher animals and then they'd have to conjure a second explanation for the quantum leap in the quality and quantity of those traits found only in the human being.

Darwinian evolution doesn't allow for quantum leaps. The Bible does, the fossil record does, the works of the world's leading paleontologist and the curator of invertebrates at the American Museum of Natural History does; studies by the people at the National Academy of Sciences, the Max Plank Institute of Biology, the Carnegie Institution for Science, the University of California at Davis, and both Stanford and Haifa Universities, along with thousands of other tenured scientists across every relevant field of science does, but Darwin's theory doesn't.

Desperate efforts to ascribe "intelligence" to Koko the gorilla who was said to have been taught a few rudimentary words or "creativity" to some or another primate because its "paintings" somewhat resemble the splatter at a murder scene, suffers the same fate upon even the slightest examination.

How these abilities first came to exist in the highly complex creatures towards the very, very end of the evolutionary process would still first need to be explained, and then there would also need to be a second explanation for the quantum leap to such seemingly divinely-inspired works as the books of Tolstoy, the statue of David, and the all-you-can-eat breakfast buffet at Harrah's.

With no explanation for where the metaphysical traits might have come from, and still as stumped as the world's very first caveman about how they might work, the Atheists score the trifecta of cluelessness in not knowing what evolutionary purpose they might serve.

If the Atheists were right about everything being merely a heartless battle for survival, then common sense would suggest that the metaphysical traits would be *anti*-evolutionary. After all, if all that matters is the material world, then any time, energy, and other resources invested in the metaphysical realm would seem to be a distraction, at best. In fact, according to Atheistic theory, someone even just playing a game of Uno could have set the whole human race back millennia.

Even more confounding to the Atheists is the fact that many of these metaphysical traits are altruistic. Altruism simply shouldn't exist in a universe that Dawkins swears is one of nothing other than "pitiless indifference."

Of course, Dawkins doesn't actually know the entire universe, but what he does know is himself. Dawkins' claim, then, seems more like a confession of his personal attitude towards others, which would go a long way towards explaining why he has no compunction about misleading the people foolish enough to believe that what he's peddling is science.

Over the years, there have been any number of attempts to try and conjure one or another clever-sounding "What if?" story in an effort to show how altruism is really just pitiless indifference in disguise, but these versions of the Atheists "Ingenious Illusions" gambit are never any more scientific than are the ones that these same Atheists use to try and explain away the same obvious design – and the same obvious designer – in the physical world.

The most commonly embraced of these wholly unsubstantiated, patently absurd, just-so stories at the moment is that "somehow" (and for no reason) luck "somehow" "just happened" to have "somehow" "just happened" to have randomly made man a "social being." Not me personally, but apparently everyone else.

It was this sociability, they say, that then led to things as stunningly unlikely and otherwise wholly inexplicable as cooperation, the division of labor and, eventually, the most inexplicable thing of all, black licorice fro-yo.

Of course, "sociability" is still yet just another one of those many, many (many, many) things that the Atheists swear doesn't exist anywhere in the universe except, you know, it "somehow" "just happens" to "somehow" exist and it "somehow" "just happens" to "somehow" exist at exactly that one time and exactly that one place that the science of Intelligent Design in general and the Bible in particular predicts, and at just that moment when yet another one of the Atheists' patently absurd theories would fall apart completely without it.

The Atheists have a bigger problem than just the scientific and statistical impossibility of the "sociability gene" having "somehow" "just happened" to have "somehow" "just happened" to have come about by random luck, though. The problem is that that very same scientific and statistical impossibility would have had to have "somehow" "just happened" to have "somehow" "just happened" *twice*…

…in just the same species…

…at just the same time…

…on just the same street!

In order for sociability to have been the trait that eventually led to advanced civilization, at least *two* members of the same species would have had to have "somehow" "just happened" to have randomly popped out the sociability gene during just the same brief lifespan, and they'd have had to have done so in close enough physical proximity to each other for them to have then gotten together to socialize.

The very first human being to have been lucky enough to have randomly popped out the primitive sociability gene who approached a still ruthless man/beast with his hand out saying "let's be friends," would have been like Steve Urkel at a Hell's Angles gathering: his genes might have survived, but chances are that they'd have been between the teeth of some guy named "Moose" (if they weren't already between the teeth of some moose named "Guy.")

The sociability gene wouldn't have rendered the first human being to have had it the *most* likely to have survived; it would have made him the *least* likely to have survived. Socializing with something that has no other purpose in life than to rip your throat out and feed you to its children wouldn't seem to be a great strategy for survival. It sure didn't help me much in my last relationship.

Actually, it's even worse than that for the Atheists. In reality, the sociability gene would have had to have "somehow" "just happened" to have "somehow" "just happened" to have randomly popped out a lot more than just twice at once; it would have had to have "somehow" "just happened" to have "somehow" "just happened" to have randomly popped out across the entire species at once.

As lovely as it surely would have been had they discovered in the fossil record that Urkel and Moose had eventually worked out their differences and moved in together, the problem would have been that the rest of the species and, in fact, the rest of the animal kingdom, would have still been just as pitilessly indifferent to their arrangement as they are to everything else. Urkel and Moose, then, wouldn't have been made any more likely to have survived by their union; in fact, they'd have been made only easier prey as they stood there gazing lovingly into each other's eyes. Things would have only been that much worse for them if they'd then decided to sit down and play a game of Uno.

The quality of sociability randomly popping out across an entire species at once may not be impossible (you know, if it wasn't impossible), but it is yet again, and as always, and as with all things, the very last thing that the Atheist hypothesis predicts. Did I say the "very last" thing? Make that the "very, very, very last" thing.

On the other hand, it is, yet again, and as always, and as with all things, the very first thing a believer would expect and something, yet again, found on the very first pages of the very first book of monotheism's very first text. In fact, the Bible not only explains where man's sociability came from, it is a manual for how best to then, socialize.

CHAPTER TWENTY

LIVE LONG AND PROSPER

Still as clueless as the world's very first caveman about its origin, how it functions, or what evolutionary purpose the metaphysical traits might serve, the Atheists' claim that sociability simply must have "somehow" "just happened" to have "somehow" "just happened" to have evolved through the Darwinian process is even further belied by the fact that what sociability produces is not survival.

Every plant and animal of every species, family, and kind alive today all survived just fine prior to the arrival of sociability and the kind of societies that man and only man has since created. If they hadn't, we wouldn't be here, and that would have really have pissed me off, since I have tickets to the Knicks game on Thursday.

The unique product that sociability allows for is something very different from – and even more anti-Darwinian than – anything that has ever come before it. What sociability allows for is prosperity and abundance.

Clearly prosperity and abundance aren't requisites for survival, which is why they say that "cheetahs never prosper." It's also why you've never seen a crocodile wearing alligator shoes or vice versa. In fact, if we humans were really just another animal species, prosperity and abundance would actually be de-evolutionary, yet again, and in still yet more ways.

Only in prosperous societies does one find such things as lethargy, sedentariness, and obesity; and that's just in Jerry Nadler. Clearly, things like lethargy, sedentariness, and obesity aren't good for the individual's chances for survival, unless they'd been hoping to be on the cover of one of *Sports Illustrated*'s new woke swimsuit editions.

Things would only have been that much worse for the first humans to have experienced prosperity and abundance since, not yet advanced, early humans would have had no place to store their excess and no way to preserve it for later. Rotting leftovers would have drawn disease and scavengers to their primitive enclaves in just the same way that San Francisco draws its population today.

One altruistic trait – charity – stands out as singularly anti-Darwinian. Charity at once makes the most fit of the species at least somewhat less fit to survive, while specifically making the least fit more likely to live on and, in turn, pass on its inferior genes.

In fact, one particular form of charity – adoption – specifically sees the most fit choosing some other member of the species' DNA to help perpetuate; that person often being the offspring of the otherwise very least fit to survive of all.

Finally, even if one were to accept the Atheists' patently absurd and wholly unsubstantiated claim that altruism is really some sort of yet to be conjured survival mechanism that the human species evolved by luck through the random interactions of insentient materials, the Atheists would still need to account for the love, compassion, and charity that human beings show towards other living things.

According to the Atheists' theory, the continued survival of other species creates competition for otherwise scarce resources and thus any effort on their behalf would seem to be, yet again, and in still yet even another series of ways, anti-Darwinian. After all, according to the Atheists, it's all nothing other than the survival of the fittest conducted with pitiless indifference on every occasion or, as it's known in Hollywood: "Hollywood."

While some may attempt to deride Western Civilization by calling it a "dog-eat-dog world," the truth is that in

Western Civilization, we don't eat our own and, in fact, we don't even eat dogs. What we actually do is put members of our own species in prison if they're even cruel to another kind.

This practice is anti-Darwinian at least twice over. It, at once, ensures the survival of a member of another species while at the same time it isolates a member of our own species in a situation where procreational opportunities are few, rarely consensual, and no matter what Facebook says, "reproductive success" is an anatomical impossibility.

The metaphysical traits in general and altruism in particular having "somehow" "just happened" to have "somehow" "just happened" to have created themselves by some more random interactions of insentient materials may not be impossible – you know, if it wasn't in each, and all, and in every known way scientifically impossible – but it's certainly not the first thing that the Atheist hypothesis predicts. It is, in fact, once again and as always, and as with all things, the very, very, very last.

Conversely, everything thus far discussed in this section on the metaphysical – altruism, sociability, prosperity, and abundance – are exactly nothing less than what one would expect from a loving God, just like the God of the Bible.

CHAPTER TWENTY-ONE

GOOD GOD!

Incapable of making a materialistic argument that can even first begin to explain the existence of the altruistic traits, the Atheists attempt to win the day by default. "Oh, yeah," they say, "If your God exists, then why is there evil in the world, heh, heh, heh?" They then usually twirl their moustaches and spit tobacco juice on the ground, which is itself a miracle, since most don't chew and only about half can even grow facial hair.

This question, however, fails the Atheists yet again. While, clearly, the existence of altruism has already disproved the Atheists' claim that only pitiless indifference exists, so too does the existence of evil. Evil is as far from indifference as is good.

Once the Atheists have acknowledged the existence of evil, they've then already conceded the existence of a creator; now all they're doing is debating personalities.

Since the theory of Intelligent Design doesn't even postulate a specific deity, much less its Q score, the science of Intelligent Design emerges from this challenge not only totally unscathed, but wholly confirmed by the Atheists themselves. Not liking something doesn't mean that that something doesn't exist. If it did, then there'd be no such thing as a Jennifer Aniston movie. In fact, not liking something actually proves that that something does exist; otherwise, there'd be nothing not to like. Duh! People who don't like things that don't exist are called "psychopaths."

Of course, the existence of evil might seem to pose a more significant challenge to those of us who believe in a God that is good, and it would, if what had been created was evil alone. It wasn't. What God (or luck) created was "good and evil." Like "up and down," good and evil is a single concept that cannot be separated and still have any meaning.

Since good cannot exist without evil, if a good God wished for there to be good in the world for His creations to then seek, enjoy and contribute to with their actions, evil would have to exist as well. Such a God could surely have created a world with neither good nor evil, but, as we shall see, thank God He didn't.

Think about it this way. When people write books, plays, movies and TV shows, we are like Gods in the act of creation. Of course, some people write *Fuller House*, too, but that's beside the point. As the ultimate authority, we writers create the laws and constants of the universes in which our characters then live, work, and play. Let's take a look at some of the things we mortals have created with this power and see what they'd have been like if evil didn't exist.

The TV show *NCIS* would be just "S" as there'd be no need for a navy, no such thing as a criminal and nothing to investigate except maybe "who brought the pie; it's just so delish?" Of course, in such a world *every* pie would be "just so delish," so the question would be moot, the conversation deadly dull and the pie would be just average. Again. In fact, it might not even be all that good a pie, since they'd have nothing to compare it to and no reason to have ever learned how to make a better one.

Without evil, *Breaking Bad* would be *Breaking Just Fine, Thanks, Why In The World Do You Ask?* There'd be no reason to call Saul and, in fact, there'd probably be no Saul to call at all. *Batman* without the Joker wouldn't have a plot; *Hamilton* without Burr wouldn't have a shot, and can you even imagine *Othello* without Iago? Why would the monkeys even bother?

Good without evil isn't good; it's nothing. It's worse than nothing; it's monotony without purpose, perspective, direction, meaning or even the hope of happiness. My God, have you never spent time with a Jehovah's Witness?

On the other hand, the existence of good *and* evil allows for literally everything that can even be imagined. It is between these parameters that one finds right and wrong, better and worse, truth and lies, winning and losing, and beauty and ugliness in all of their permutations, combinations, and degrees.

There's a reason that the symbol of the arts – the profession where we humans have the unlimited power of creation – isn't the pie tin. Neither is it the face of just good. It is, in fact, the *twin* faces of good and evil – comedy and tragedy – because even back three thousand years ago, when Jon Voight starred in the very first performance at the Aeschylus theater in ancient Greece, it was understood that it is between these parameters that *every* story can be told, and that without one, there simply is no the other.

The Atheists, of course, can't even entertain, much less answer, the question as to why the universe would have created good and evil since reason and randomness are opposites. It's just yet another one of those many, many

(many, many) things that the Atheists swear doesn't exist anywhere in the universe and which would totally debunk their in each and all and in every way, both scientifically and statistically impossible origin myth if it did, that "somehow" "just happens" to exist and it "somehow" "just happens" to exist right here, right now, and in just that one place that the science of Intelligent Design in general and the Bible in particular predicts.

The believer, on the other hand, can once again not only answer this first and most essential of all human questions, but he can do so once again based on all known observation, discovery, and experiment – you know, what real scientists call "data" – from over the course of the entirety of all of human experience.

If there is a good God like the God of the Bible, then He'd have created good and evil for the very same reason that literally every known intelligent lifeform that has ever had the power of creation does: it would be to thrill and amaze, awe and delight, entertain, enlighten, and inspire an audience that is capable of understanding and appreciating the show. Duh!

God (or luck) didn't create evil; God (or luck) created *everything* that can even be imagined and, in turn, that gives our lives purpose, perspective, direction, meaning and the chance to pursue our own happiness and to help bring happiness to others.

Meanwhile, just as much can be learned about something by its absence as by its presence. If it is God that created good and evil, then one would expect for such things as purpose, perspective, direction, meaning, and happiness to be missing from those places where God's influence has been expunged from society. This is, in fact, exactly what we find today. Man, do we find it!

In *Hollowed Out: A Warning About America's Next Generation*, recent California Teacher of the Year Jeremy Adams, describes the condition of the children who are being raised in this era of growing Militant Atheist control. He wrote:

> *[These children] are utterly destitute in the realm of what we might call "human flourishing" – fulfilling the timeless aspirations and deepest yearnings of the human soul: to love, to know, to honor, to serve, to lead.*

This is how *Sixty Minutes* began a recent report on the state of America's young in today's Militant Atheist era:

> *The U.S. surgeon general has called it an "urgent public health crisis" – a devastating decline in the mental health of kids across the country. According to the CDC, the rates of suicide, self-harm, anxiety and depression*

are up among adolescents – a trend that began before the pandemic.

Feel free to throw in the epidemics of homelessness, drug addiction, and incompetence across every major field of basic education and even rudimentary skills – all of which correlate to perfection, both logically and chronologically, with the rise, spread, and now empowerment of the Militant Atheist movement – and you'll have only touched the surface of what these children are suffering through now that the Militants have so successfully expunged God's influence from their lives.

There's still yet one more epidemic undeniably associated with the Militant Atheist movement of today. The children raised in the Militant Atheist era are not only just hurting and killing themselves; they are hurting and killing each other.

In a 2019 article published in *Townhall*, Dennis Prager distilled the data compiled by Grant Duwe, Ph. D. and the author of *Mass Murder* in *the United States: A History*:

In the 20th century, every decade before the 1970s had fewer than 10 mass public shootings. In the 1950s, for example, there was one mass shooting. And then a steep rise began. In the 1960s, there were six mass shootings. In the 1970s, the number rose to 13. In the 1980s, the number increased 2 1/2 times, to 32. And it rose again in the 1990s, to 42. As for this century, The New York Times reported in 2014 that, according to the FBI, "Mass shootings have risen drastically in the past half-dozen years."

Murder isn't new. In fact, I think I recall reading something about one that took place when there were still only four people in the entire world. Guns in America aren't new; in fact, long before schools were turned into "gun free zones," America's public schools routinely allowed guns on campuses for training and a wide variety of shooting competitions. Human nature hasn't changed; so, what has?

The answer is again simple and obvious. When people claiming scientific authority decree that human life is in no objective, qualitative way above that of the flea, you just might start producing people who believe that human life is in no objective, qualitative way above that of the flea. Duh!

When John Lennon did nothing more than put the Militant Atheist political doctrine to music in the song, "Imagine," he laid out the Militant Atheists' utopian promise. A world without God, they swore, would be a peaceful paradise, because there would be "Nothing to kill or die for." The part the Militants don't tell their victims is that, a world with nothing to kill or die for, is also a world with nothing to live for. And no reason *not* to kill.

If it is belief in God that has given the human being literally everything that can even be imagined, then it is only to be expected that, where the Militants have succeeded in expunging belief in God from society, there is nothing left to even think about. In fact, in the Militant Atheist era, some kids can't even imagine a reason to go on living.

CHAPTER TWENTY-TWO

THE PURPOSE OF MILITANT ATHEISM

At this point, the question simply must be asked: why do the Militants do it? Why is it so important to the people behind this movement that others not believe in God, that they are willing to betray their professions, lie to those who trust them the most, peddle patent absurdities as "settled science" and knowingly inflict on successive generations of the young, virtually every existential horror that can even be imagined? To find the answer, one must only know what Militant Atheism is, and the purpose it's served for other ideologies and revolutions before the Woke revolution of today.

While atheism as a personal belief has likely been around for as long as we humans have walked the earth; Militant Atheism – the aggressive attempt to enforce non-belief on a societal level – is still fairly new to the modern world.

In fact, it only first gained intellectual credence a mere hundred-fifty years ago, when Karl Marx published his *Communist Manifesto.*

It would take about another fifty years for the first Militant Atheist regime to come to power and, in just the one-hundred years since, Militant Atheism has been a central part of numerous ideological efforts – none of them good – including: Leninism, Stalinism, Hitlerism, Maoism, and now "Wokeism."

The fact that there have been ideological differences between these political movements is irrelevant, because Militant Atheism is not a political belief. Militant Atheism is simply a weapon used by ideologues, demagogues, and revolutionaries to clear away all moral obstacles to their path to power and the ungodly way they then intend to rule.

If you think that the comparison of Wokeism to the bloodiest regimes in all of human history seems a tad over-wrought – perhaps a bit of hyperbole by a Bible-thumping author trying to stir up some controversy – consider the fact that it was Bill Maher, well-known for his own aggressive disdain for religious believers, who made the comparison first.

On a recent segment of his show, *Real Time,* Maher went down the long list of similarities that Wokeism has with

Leninism and Stalinism, checking off every box along the way. Then he had this to say about Wokeism and Maoism:

> *Yesterday, I asked ChatGPT, "Are there any similarities between Mao's 'Cultural Revolution' of the 1960s and the Woke Revolution of today?" And it wrote back, "How much time do you have?"*

One suspects that Maher only left out Nazism because the singular evils of their methods and the pure horror of their specific tactics has rendered comparing anything to Nazism beyond the pale for some. Not the Woke, of course. They compare *everything* to Nazism, you know, except the closest thing there is to Nazism today, Islamicism, which they applaud with gusto and cheer on, hoping for more.

The specific comparisons between Wokeism and the other Militant Atheist movements of the past hundred years could fill a book, and, in fact they do. It was my previous book, *The Woke Supremacy: An Antisocialist Manifesto.*

Just some of these similarities include the perversion of language, the demonizing of dissent and, of course, people who called themselves "scientists" who have a "prior commitment" to an ideological cause that leads them to lie, lie big, lie often, and lie as simply a matter of course.

The most important of these similarities for our purpose here is that, whatever the ideological differences between the Militant Atheist movements might or might not have been, every one of them, from Day One through today, makes it followers the very same fundamental promise, and they all promise to accomplish it through the very same means.

Whether it was Leninism, Stalinism, Hitlerism, Maoism, or Wokeism (or any of the less "accomplished" efforts like Kimism in North Korea or Castroism in Cuba), they all promise that, if the people will turn away from the God that they embrace and embrace *them* as the new Gods, they will create the perfect world. In fact, they all promise to do so in the very same way: by using the powers of government to engineer an entirely new, never-before-seen kind of human being.

What this newly engineered human being would be like differed according to the ideology, but they all promised to use the powers of indoctrination, strict enforcement, and the more heavy-handed means afforded them by government control, to create the perfect human specimen.

The communists, for example, promised the people that, if they embraced them as Gods, they would bring about a "workers' paradise" by using their powers to create a human being who was wholly devoid of self-interest. This never-before-seen kind of human being would toil hard, and always to the best of his abilities, asking for himself only the bare minimum in return.

The Nazis promised their followers that, if they turned away from the God that they embraced and, instead, embrace the Nazis as Gods, these new Gods would use their powers to engineer the never-before-seen human being who is totally devoid of human emotions. The new Nazi creation would produce unparalleled prosperity and abundance, as the individual's productivity and performance would be unhampered by such frivolous and costly distractions as love, empathy, compassion, or the fear of regret.

The all-new, never-before-seen kind of human being the Gods of the Woke promise to engineer is one that is wholly devoid of "hate." Through indoctrination, strict enforcement and the more heavy-handed means available to them once they've come to power, the Woke promise to create the perfect world where only love exists.

Over the years, these various Gods took on a variety of names. In communist regimes, the all-knowing, all-loving, all-powerful Gods were called "The State" or "The Party." In Nazi, Germany, they called their all-knowing, all-loving and all-powerful God, "Der Fuhrer." In his amalgamation of the four Militant Atheist regimes of his lifetime, Orwell called the all-knowing, all-loving and all-powerful God of Oceania, "Big Brother." Today's version of Militant Atheism calls their all-knowing, all-loving, all-powerful God, "The Science."

Of course, what these God of Wokeism don't tell their followers is that, other than in totalitarian regimes, there's no such thing as "The Science" and that what they're peddling as the "gospel," is well-known to them to be patently absurd, wholly unsubstantiated, "just-so" stories that extravagantly fail in their every test.

The adherence to this new religion of Wokeism are so dedicated to their Gods, that mere skepticism is a blasphemy and dissent is punishable by a means of "cancellation," more technologically advance – and thus less bloody – than the ones employed by their predecessors, but meant to accomplish the very same ends.

CHAPTER TWENTY-THREE

ALL YOU NEED IS LOVE
(BUT ALL THEY HAVE IS HATE)

Truth be known, these new Gods known as "The Science," have done an outstanding job of engineering the never-before-seen human being that they promised. In fact, one can track how, along with the rise, spread and now empowerment of today's Militant Atheists, hate has more and more disappeared from the thinking of succeeding generations. In fact, it is now barely detectable amongst the latest iterations of those born into this latest Militant Atheist era.

The problem is that, since like "good and evil" and "up and down," love and hate is a single concept that cannot be separated and still have any meaning. By succeed in eliminating hate from the lives of their young victims; the Militants have succeeded in create successive generation wholly incapable of love.

Without love or hate – or any of its permutations, combinations and degrees – the professional Atheists have succeeded in creating the all-new, never-before-seen kind of human being who is utterly indifferent to anything and everything.

These children don't seek to love, to know, to serve, to honor, or to lead, for the simple reason that they've been rendered wholly indifferent to love and knowledge and uninterested in knowing what is and isn't worthy of service and honor. They don't seek to lead, because their Gods of Wokeism have convinced them that there is simply nowhere special to go.

It's not that these children are wholly without passion; it's that their only passion is for indifference. Thus, they might feel passionately about such policies as open borders and sanctuary cities, but these policies are not based on love for the migrants – they don't even know the migrants, so how can they love them?

Instead, the young Woke "passionately" support the policies the demagogues and revolutionaries push for their own nefarious purposes, wholly out of indifference to the next victims of the drug-runners, child-traffickers, and terrorists these policies allow into the country wholly unchecked, right alongside those who might truly be in need. The Woke don't love the migrants; they just don't hate drug-runners, child-traffickers, or terrorists.

Similarly, the Woke might be "passionate" in their support of drag queens performing for small children; but it is not out of love for the drag queens. They don't even know them; so how can the possibly love them? Instead, this passion stems entirely from the Woke's utter indifference to the destruction of a child's innocence. The Woke don't love drag queens; they just don't hate destroying a child's innocence.

The young Woke don't support the Nazi-like terror group Hamas because they love Hamas. They don't even know them, so how can they love them? Instead, the young victims of the Militants support Hamas entirely out of indifference towards the suffering of their Jewish victims. They don't love Hamas; they just don't hate rape, torture, and terror.

Proof of the Woke's indifference is found in the fact that, while they may be passionate – often even aggressive – they have not spent even one moment to look into the issues to ensure that they are on the side of the good and the right. In the world the Militant Atheists have created without God, there simply is no such thing as the good and the right.

With the Woke revolutionaries having succeeded in changing the definition of "love" to now mean only indifference; they have thus succeeded in changing the definition of "hate" to mean "anyone and everyone who has ever lived and everything they have ever said, done, or created." Other than that, though, the victims of the Militants don't hate anyone or anything.

Prior to the arrival of the new Gods, and their having engineered this new, never-before-seen perfect human being wholly devoid of hate, everyone was a "hater" and everything they said, did and created was a product of that hate.

The Woke are so totally convinced of this, in fact, that they can neither even fathom any other explanation nor do they even feel the need to try. The Woke's hatred for everyone and everything that came before them is because, just as with every other Militant Atheist movement; history is divided into two parts: everything that came before the arrival of their new Gods is evil; and everything after their arrival and their having engineered the perfect human being is good. That's what they mean by calling themselves "woke." Their new Gods have "awakened" them to The Truth.

The great revelation of the new Gods of Wokeism is that nothing is objectively, qualitatively better than anything else. Therefore, in the gospel of Wokeism, anyone who ever loved anything could only be a "bigot" and anyone who ever hated anything, could only be a "phobic." In fact, when the Militants and their followers call someone a "supremacist," all that they mean is that they believe that something can be objectively, qualitatively superior to something else.

The Woke are so filled with hate for everyone who has ever lived, that they can't even conceive of the possibility that even one of them might have ever said or done anything good or important from which they might learn.

The hate everyone who has ever lived so much, that, in their minds they turned everyone from the past into a mythic beast with such superhuman powers that, to merely hear their voice, read their words or merely glimpse their visage on a statue or painting threatens to take over their minds and turn them into "haters," themselves.

So purely evil is everyone and everything from prior to the arrival of their new Gods, that every hint of their having once existed needs to be fully expunged from the world until only "love" remains.

The utopian promise that the Militant Atheists make this time around is that, without hate, the world will be filled with only love. What the Militants have delivered to their victims, though, is a world wholly without love.

The world the Militants have created for their victims exists only between the parameters of hatred and indifference; with the Woke passionately hating the "haters" (i.e. everyone else who has ever lived) and wholly indifferent to anything and everything else.

Proof that the Woke world exists only between the parameters of hatred and indifference is found in the fact that, neither the new Gods nor their worshipers, ever even attempt to argue for what it is they believe in in the affirmative.

Like the Militant Atheist "scientists" with regard to the Big Question, they can ridicule and assault the beliefs of others (and bully people into submission); but when it comes time for them to offer an argument on behalf of what it is they believe in its stead, the Woke can silence, bully, intimidate, shout and call names; but what they can't do is reasonably and rationally lay out their own positions.

The reason that the Woke never attempt to argue for their beliefs in the affirmative is simple: since, like the Militant Atheist "scientists," they don't have any beliefs; there is simply nothing for them to affirm. Atheism is all about destruction; it does not and cannot ever build.

Even when Lennon did nothing more than to put the Militant Atheist doctrine to music in the song, "Imagine," all he could do was call for the elimination of various things. Without God, countries or possessions, he promised, the world would be a perfect place; but, when it came time to discuss the actual mechanics of how such a world would operate, all he could do was say, "Just use your imagination."

This, of course, is the same thing that the professional Atheist "scientists" do. They use their wiles and the cachet of their titles to argue against the existence of God but, when it comes time for them to argue on behalf of what it is that they say they believe about the origin and design of the universe, they are forced to imagine bowls of magic soup, monkeys floating through the cosmos typing Elizabethan poetry and horny aliens from outer space who then had sex with a rock.

CHAPTER TWENTY-FOUR

NO GOD, NO SCIENCE, NO LOVE...NO SEX?

With today's Militants having succeeded in expunging all love from their young victims' worldview; they've succeeded in expunging it from their personal lives, as well. In fact, having been convinced that nothing is in any way objectively, qualitatively better than anything else, the victims of the Atheists don't even seek to find anything to love.

The victims of the Militants don't seek out great art or great literature for the simple reason that, in the Militant Atheist world, it has been decreed by the new Gods that goodness and greatness doesn't exist.

Telling, then, is the fact that these children literally hold in their hands more access to the great works of art and literature than any ten thousand "privileged" kings, and tsars, and popes of yore combined, and yet they seek out only the trivial, the banal, and the profane.

Even more telling, though, is that those who are in those positions of authority that had been, from the dawn of civilization until right up until, literally, the very second of the Militant Atheist takeover, specifically charged with introducing the next generation to the good and the great, and stoking their love for the better, not only don't teach their victims about the great works, but they go out of their way to keep them hidden from their victims and to denigrate them once they've been found.

Thus, college professors who, from the very inception of the university, had been charged with introducing the next generation to the great works of literature which, together, have come to be known as the "classics," now dismiss these works as the product of "haters," and do everything in their power to prevent their young victims from reading them.

Since the world the Militant Atheists seek to create for their young victims lies only between the parameters of hatred and indifference; with the professional Atheists having succeeded in denying their young victims the good and the great to love; they cannot provide anything for them to love in its stead.

Thus, at the same time that the Militants have succeeded in expunging the great works of literature from the schools' curricula; they have more and more replaced these lessons with programs designed for no other purpose than to give their victims more reason to hate.

Thus, along with the demise of courses in Shakespeare, Chaucer and the Bible, for example, one finds the rise of newly-invented, wholly-bogus classes in such things as "ethnic" and "gender" studies. The young victims of the Atheists lap up these lessons because, with its having been decreed that nothing is objectively, qualitatively better than anything else, "racism" and "sexism" and other "bigotries" and "phobias" are the only possible explanation for anything that has ever been said, done, thought or created.

In the end, then, the children can either hate the classics for being "bigoted" or they can be indifferent to the classics but the one thing they'll not have done is to have actually read the classics or, in fact, anything else that was written or created prior to the arrival of the new Gods and their having engineered the Woke.

These classes in how and why to hate are no more historically accurate than are the claims the Militant Atheists make in their patently absurd, wholly unsubstantiated, and extravagantly failed origin myth. Like the Atheist origin myth, it is no secret that the "history" the Militants are teaching is bogus and that the Militant Atheist "historian" has the same "prior commitment" as do their co-ideologists in fields like "evolutionary biology."

In fact, long before I had any idea that I'd be writing this work about the evils of Militant Atheism, I began my first book, *The KinderGarden of Eden: How the Modern Liberal Thinks*, with the following quotation from Howard Zinn.

Zinn is the de facto official historian of this latest Militant Atheist movement and thus, his book, *A People's History of the United States*, is the single most assigned text in the primary schools and colleges now under the Militants' control. Zinn decreed that "Objectivity is undesirable." He then went on to explain why objective facts are "undesirable" to this – and every – Militant Atheist movement:

> *If you think that history should serve a social purpose – that it should in some way advance the causes of humanity – then you make your choices [as to what to claim to be true] based on that.*

Objectivity is only undesirable if one's goal is to spread lies. If one's purpose is to seek the truth, however, objectivity is not only desirable; it is utterly essential. In fact, seeking to ensure objectivity is the entire reason that scientists – real scientists – created the Scientific

Method. It is the reason that schools and universities used to have what were called "academic standards." It is also why the Militant Atheists not only reject but must reverse the Scientific Method and why, today, "academic standards" is an oxymoron.

Zinn, of course, is far from alone in his belief that history should be falsified in order to "advance the causes of humanity." In fact, it is a belief shared by literally every propagandist from the previous Militant Atheist regimes. The Leninists, the Stalinists, the Hitlerists, and the Maoists propagandists like Leni Riefenstahl, *all* believed that they were "advancing the causes of humanity" by falsifying history.

Here's a pretty good rule of thumb. When you belong to a movement where the leading "scientists" and most assigned "historian" all admit that they're lying and they then even tell you why; it's a pretty good bet that you're on the wrong side of history and that you don't really believe in (or even care about) science.

One thing that has struck me from the beginning of my journey is how often the Militant Atheists come right out and admit that they lie, lie big, lie often, and lie as simply a matter of course. You would think this might be something they'd want to keep hidden from their followers. The Militant Atheists, however, know that they don't need to keep their lies quiet, because they know that their followers neither love truth nor hate lies.

With the Atheists having eliminated the greatest stories ever told; the only storytellers that their young victims know all live and work in Hollywood and, like the Militant Atheist "scientists" and "historians," they, too, have a "prior commitment" to the political jihad known as "wokeism."

The Militant Atheist "entertainer" is no more of an entertainer than the Militant Atheist "scientist" is a scientist or the Militant Atheist "historian" is a historian. He, too, is someone who merely uses his profession to "advance the causes of humanity" according to the Militant Atheist doctrine (no matter which of the Militant Atheist ideologies he worships.)

Almost entirely gone from the tales now told by the powers-that-be in Hollywood, then, are the everyday heroes – those who do not possess superpowers and therefore can be emulated – whose heroism comes from their goodness and decency. Goodness and decency simply do not fall into the parameters of hatred and indifference that is the entirety of the Woke universe.

Rare, then, is the *Casablanca*, where a jaded saloon-keeper steps up and does the right thing or the *It's a Wonderful Life*, where the message is that one is a hero to those around them when they live a life of simple goodness. Self-sacrifice is simply not a noble concept in the eyes of the Militants' victims since, given that nothing is in any way better than anything else, there is simply nothing worth sacrificing for.

With the Militant Atheists having expunged true heroes from their stories, they have nothing good or great with which to replace them. Unsurprising, then, is that, in place of true heroes; the Militant Atheist era has seen the rise, spread and now ubiquity of the *anti*hero.

Starting with Michael Corleone (*Godfather II*) and *Scarface* and leading today to characters like Tony Soprano, Frank Underwood (*House of Cards*), and Walter White of *Breaking Bad*, the "heroes" of the Militant Atheists all live in the same universe of hatred and indifference that the Militants have created for their young victims.

Whether it was Corleone, Scarface, Soprano, Underwood, White or others; they all live in a universe that exists only between the parameters of hatred for their rivals and utter indifference towards the innocent victims who get caught up in their war for more money and power. They live in the universe that Dawkins envisions and Trivers has decreed, where there is nothing but the pitiless indifference of the insentient and the "survival of the fittest" of Darwinism.

Telling about these shows, is that their creators are amongst the only known beings in this universe with the God-like powers of creation. They are free to create any universe they can imagine and populate it with any creatures their hearts desire and yet they cannot even fathom a world where goodness, greatness and love exists. Either they can't fathom it; or they don't want their young victims to know that such a world is within their grasp.

Meanwhile, the other form of storytelling that had always been a means of introducing the next generation to the good and the great, popular music and its poetic lyrics, has seen the Militants achieve equal success in their efforts to expunge the good, right and beautiful.

Love songs are now regularly deemed "internalized misogyny" – a concept wholly fabricated by the demagogues for their use in those courses in how and why to hate – while the vile, the vulgar, and the heartless are now called "liberating." In fact, *Complex* magazine (controlled by the evil folks at *BuzzFeed*) called Cardi B.'s loveless, "Wet A** P***y," "The epitome of women's empowerment."

Complex was far from alone in their efforts to promote the vile, vulgar, and loveless. In fact, everyone from the once cutting-edge *Rolling Stone* magazine to the chardonnay-swilling, above-it-all elitists at *NPR* passed over every other song from the previous twelve months to laud "WAP" as the "best song" of the year.

What made this the "best" song to those who do not believe in good and evil or any of its permutations, combinations and degrees, is that, in the Militant Atheist era, love is self-hatred and emotional indifference is self-love.

The reason for this is simple: to believe that one's life might be better with another person means that one isn't satisfied with themselves. Since the Militant Atheist decree is that the Woke have been engineered to be perfect, then to seek anything better proves that one must be prejudiced against themselves.

The fact that Militant Atheism lies only between the parameters of hatred and indifference is further evidenced by the one and only truly new artform to have come out of the Militant Atheist era, "Gangsta rap."

Gangsta rap is an entire genre where there is only hatred for one's rivals and pitiless indifference towards anyone and everyone else. It is all about "the survival of the fittest" with no love to be found anywhere. Is it any surprise, then, that in the Militant Atheist world, Jeffrey Epstein is their hero? Is it any surprise, then, that when he could no longer do them any good; they had their hero whacked?

Since Wokeism decrees that we humans are in no objective, qualitative way above the animals, it is unsurprising to find that the Militants have succeeded in expunging the singularly human from all interpersonal relationships. Towards this end, the professional Atheists have succeeded in reducing love between two people to the mere fornication of random beasts.

Nowhere to be found in the world the Militants' have created for their victims are such "pre-Woke" notions as courtship, romance, chivalry, and commitment. In fact, such things are now taught to be proof of one's self-hatred. The mutual self-sacrifice previously recognized as essential to turning two individuals into a single loving couple, is now considered to be all the evidence that is need to prove that one hasn't been engineered properly.

Since Militant Atheism doesn't allow for anything positive to fill the void; the death of romance that correlates to perfection, both logically and chronologically, to the rise, spread and now empowerment of the Militant Atheist doctrine has seen the rise, spread and now ubiquity of heartless – and often violent – pornography and soulless Tinder "dating," leaving the very best that a young victim of the Militants can hope for by way of personal intimacy being sexual "benefits" provided by mere friends, where even the hope of anything more meaningful has been written out of the contract even before the mechanical processes have begun.

With the professional Atheists having succeeded in leaving their victims without beauty to enjoy, heroes to admire and lovers with whom to partner; the Militants have also succeeded in making sure that their victims are wholly without friendships.

In this version of Militant Atheism, people don't have buddies, pals, allies or partners. At best, they have a cadre of people they don't even much like (thus the need for the newly coined word, "Frenemies"), who they hang out with for no other reason than that they've known each other the longest.

Proof that these children have nothing that bonds them is found in the fact that, even when they're sitting face-to-face, none of them are even looking at (much less talking to) each other. Every one of them has their face buried in their cellphones, desperately searching for something – anything – better than the people that they're with at the moment.

Those who blame the Woke's indifference to the world around them on their fixation with social media, have cause and effect reversed. They're not indifferent to the world around them because they're fixated on social media; they're fixated on social media because the Militant

Atheists have left them wholly indifferent to the world around them.

Thus, along with the Militant Atheist epidemics of suicide, homicide, depression, self-harm, anxiety, mental illness, homelessness, drug-addiction, and the others, go ahead and add what the CDC calls the "loneliness epidemic."

This is from a 2019 article from *Psychology Today* and, if one is tempted to blame the loneliness epidemic on the coronavirus hysteria and the overwrought reaction to it that saw the Militants succeed in shutting the children out of the classrooms, the article was published a full year before even the first coronavirus case was diagnosed in America:

> *MDLinx, a news service for physicians, reports "The newest epidemic in America now affects up to 47% of adults—double the number affected a few decades ago."*

A "few decades ago," of course, is exactly when the new Gods first started coming to power in the schools, universities, newsrooms, and movie and TV studios and first began to inflict their various epidemics on their young victims.

Loneliness has, of course, always been a reality. The difference is that, throughout history and right up until the very moment of the Militant Atheist takeover, loneliness had almost exclusively been an ailment suffered by the elderly. This is understandable, given that the elderly have likely lost many of their friends to death, while the physical realities of aging have likely left them less able to get out and about to socialize.

The Militant Atheists, however, have succeeded in turning loneliness into an epidemic amongst the young. In fact, the *Psychology Today* article concludes:

> *Generation Z (those born after about 1995) was found to be the loneliest generation.*

The problem is not that those under the age of thirty don't have peers with whom they can socialize. In fact, there are more people from Gen Z than from even the Baby Boomer generation. Nor has it gotten harder to socialize; in fact, thanks to technology, it's never been easier.

The problem for the victims of today's Atheists isn't that they don't have people their age to socialize with or that they not getting out to see them. See if you can spot the problem in this line from the report in *Psychology Today*:

> *In all the findings, a lack of meaningful human connectedness is paramount.*

The young victims of the Militants are connected – in fact, they're more connected than any other people in all of human history. The problem is that the Militant Atheists have succeeded in expunging all meaning from their lives.

Throughout history – as in, from the dawn of civilization right up until the very second of the Militant Atheist takeover – meaningful friendships were based on common values and shared interests. In the world the Militants have created for their victims, though, there is simply nothing of particular value for them to share nor anything of particular interest for them to pursue together as friends.

In fact, since the world the Militants have created for their victims exists only between the parameters of hatred and indifference, the *only* "value" that they can even possibly share is hatred for everything that is or ever was; and the only common interest they can possibly have is working towards its destruction. Atheism simply cannot build; Atheism can only destroy. This point is well-documented in my friend Barak Lurie's book, which he gave the ingenious title, *Atheism Destroys*.

Finally, with the Militants having succeeded in destroying the bonds between their victims and God, country, beauty, heroism, lovers, and friends, there is just one more relationship that the Militant Atheists – no matter which incarnation – must destroy in order to ensure that their power is total and unquestioned: the bond between the parent and the child.

In the Militant Atheist era, children don't have parents. Ask the Woke parent, and they'll tell you that their child is their "best friend." Of course, given the definition of "friendship" in the Militant Atheist era, even that's not saying very much.

Since in the Militant Atheist era, the adult is in no way recognized as objectively, qualitatively above the child, the Woke adult has no more right to instruct – much less discipline – the child than does any of his other peers. This, in fact, is true of all adults, including teachers, police officers and others.

Since, in a world where nothing is considered in any way different or better than anything else, the knowledge, wisdom, and experience the adult possesses holds no currency, and thus, the five-year-old's beliefs are considered to be just as right and just as valid as any adults'.

Whereas, in days of yore – and by "yore" I mean from the dawn of civilization right up until the very moment of the Militant Atheist takeover – if a child said to his parents that he thought he was a cat; it was the parents' job to clear up his confusion, show him a picture of a cat and point out the objective, qualitative differences between them such, oh, a cat's having four legs, a tail, and fur.

In the world of the Militant Atheist, however, words – like everything else – simply have no meaning (see Orwell, George for further details), and thus, the job of the parent is now nothing other than to support the child's delusions. If the child "identifies" as a cat, then he *is* a cat and the parents' only job is to then be good citizens and have their child spayed or neutered.

While the professional Atheists have convinced the parents that allowing their children to be fed multiple cocktails of untested drugs designed for no other purpose than to permanently prevent the child's natural maturation and giving the go-ahead for the Militant Atheists to perform the most savage and grisly of operations invented for no other reason than to permanently mutilate the genitals of small children is "love," it is, in fact, nothing more than the Woke parents' utter indifference to the health and welfare of their child. In their world, it has been decreed by the Gods, that there simply is no objective, qualitative difference between chopping off a young child's sex organs and not chopping off a young child's sex organs, so there's nothing for their parent to even think about.

Just how little regard the Woke have for knowledge, wisdom, and experience is evidenced not only by the parents' utter indifference to the consequences of the procedures the professional Atheists perform on their small children, but even more so by the fact that the Woke parents leave it up to the five-year-old to decide.

Now that the age of five has become the age of consent for medical decisions; it is only a matter of time until the Militants turn it into the age of consent for other things, as well. Why do you think it's so important to them that children learn about sexual proclivities and sexual activities at such an early age? After all, if there is no objective, qualitative difference between the two, they why shouldn't adults have sex with small children?

If the hypothesis being tested is that it is God that gave humanity everything, then one would expect that, where God's influence has been expunged from society, the people will have been left with nothing. This is, in fact, exactly what we find.

Today's victims of the Militant Atheists not only don't have God, they don't have science, they don't have heroes, the don't have beauty, they don't have friends, they don't have parents, and they don't have lovers. In fact, as the Militants continue to consolidate their power, more and more of them don't even have their own genitals anymore.

Meanwhile, to have accomplished this, all the professional Atheists have had to do is use their positions of authority to peddle what they, themselves, acknowledge are patently absurd, wholly unsubstantiated "just-so" stories that have extravagantly failed in their every test. Just some of these tests over the past hundred years include Leninism, Stalinism, Hitlerism and Maoism and now we can add the utter devastation of Wokeism.

Not only is God's existence supported by every known law and constant across every known field of science, as well as literally every observation, discovery and experiment – you know, what real scientists call "data" – then, but it is also now proved yet again in its negation.

Whenever and wherever the Militants have succeeded in expunging God's influence from society; the result has been exactly what those who believe in the God of the Bible would expect: a world without truth, beauty, love, compassion or justice. Even more telling, though, is the fact that these societies have been exactly what the Atheists themselves predict.

Dawkins understood that, in a world where God doesn't exist, there is and can only be pitiless indifference; while Trivers understood that, in a world without God, human life can have no more value than that of a flea. Unsurprisingly, then, every Militant Atheist movement has been pitilessly indifferent to the suffering it inflicts upon both its hatred rivals and the innocents caught up in their crossfire; while every Militant Atheist society has deemed human life to be so without value that murder, mass starvation and genocide have simply been business as usual.

Not only is a loving, monotheistic God the only possible scientific explanation for the creation and design of the material things in our universe, then, but such a God is also the only possible scientific explanation for the existence of our altruistic traits and everything that is good, right, beautiful, just and true in the world.

In the universe the Militant Atheists theorize, the altruistic traits simply shouldn't exist. It is unsurprising, then, that in the universes the Militant Atheists have used their powers to create; they don't.

NOTES

I have opted not to include footnotes in this work because, well, this isn't the year 1202 and my sources aren't hidden away in some dark, dank and dusty old cloister. In virtually every case, I provided the source of my claims in the body of the text. If there are times when I have failed to do so – or you wish to find further confirmation of my arguments – feel free to do what the kids today call a "Goggle search."

ACKNOWLEDGEMENTS

Nothing in life can be well-accomplished without friends, and this book is no exception. I have no doubt that I am indebted to others and I apologize in advance for those I might have left out.

First, I need to thank Endre Balogh for his friendship, wisdom, and the cover design for this book. I also need to thank Bob and Carrie Zeidman for their friendship, wisdom, and technical advice. Thanks as well to Mark Tapson for editorial input and a willingness to read and reread my multiple attempts to get this book right, and Barak Lurie for his guidance and assistance at every turn.

Special thanks go out to my dear friends Bettina and Jimmy Langlais for the love, friendship, and hospitality they afforded me; Virginia and Tim Scott for loving me and looking after my health and, more importantly, my soul.

Thank you to Kathleen Lieberman for her love and friend-ship (and matzo brei) and Bob and Joanne Moses for be-ing just so darn loveable. Trevor Loudon, Frank Gaffney, and Mark Anthony also deserve thanks for being my dear friends as well as loyal and trusted supporters with a big check-plus to Nick Adams for blowing just a little extra smoke whenever he thinks I need it. Thanks, as well, to Jeff Wayne, for being the consummate friend and mensch and to Carrolle Mendenhall for being an objectively, qualitatively superior human being.

Others who provided support and to whom I am grateful include, Dr. Karen Siegemund, Ph. D., Debbie Georgatos, Fini Goodman, Janis and Bill Corsair, as well as others who have told me that they simply prefer not to be mentioned by name!

And the most special thanks, from beginning to end – literally – to my family.

www.ingramcontent.com/pod-product-compliance
Lightning Source LLC
Chambersburg PA
CBHW050723260726

48661CB00001B/43